From Dictatorship to Democracy

FROM DICTATORSHIP TO DEMOCRACY

A Conceptual Framework
for Liberation

Gene Sharp

GREEN PRINT
HOUSMANS

First published in Bangkok in 1993
by the Committee for the Restoration of Democracy in Burma.
This edition first published 2011 by Housmans Bookshop and
reprinted by Green Print, an imprint of
The Merlin Press Ltd., 6 Crane Street Chambers, Crane Street,
Pontypool NP4 6ND, Wales
in association with Housmans Bookshop, 5 Caledonian Road,
King's Cross, London N1 9DX, UK

Preface © Michael Randle

ISBN. 978-1-85425-104-6

Cover image by Nick Bygon

British Library Cataloguing in Publicaation Data
is available from the British Library

Printed in the UK by Imprint Digital, Exeter

Preface to the 2011 Housmans edition of
From Dictatorship to Democracy

It is fitting that Housmans should be reprinting this influential monograph by Gene Sharp on how a society can remove a dictatorship and establish a genuine democracy through nonviolent action, or "people power".

I first met Gene Sharp in 1955 when he was assistant editor of *Peace News*, a publication, then as now, closely linked to Housmans. His 1956 lecture series, "Nonviolence and Social Change", influenced the embryonic direct action movement of the period. He provided advice and guidance to the Direct Action Committee Against Nuclear War, organisers of the historic Easter 1958 Aldermaston March against nuclear weapons - it was Sharp who drafted the briefing leaflet for the march, setting out its proposed nonviolent discipline. In 1959, *Peace News* published his first pamphlet on nonviolent resistance, *Tyranny Could Not Quell Them*, a study of the non-co-operation of teachers in occupied Norway which defeated Quisling's attempt to introduce Nazi doctrines into the Norwegian school syllabus. Sharp also contributed to another significant *Peace News* publication in the field, *Civilian Defence*, 1964, edited by Adam Roberts.

Through his subsequent writings and lectures, Sharp has established himself as one of the world's leading scholars and exponents of nonviolent action. But he has not been satisfied solely with contributing to academic discourse; he has engaged, directly or indirectly, with democratic movements facing dictatorship or oppression in many places, including the Baltic states and Eastern European countries during the Soviet period, China at the time of the Tiananmen Square demostrations, Burma, Serbia, and elsewhere. And now, in 2011, his insights have been used in Egypt, where the unarmed insurrection – together with that in Tunisia – has proved inspirational to others suffering from corrupt authoritarian regimes in the Arab world and beyond.

In pursuit of this engagement the Albert Einstein Institution, which Sharp founded in Boston in 1983, has produced a series of monographs, including the present one, to promote a deeper understanding of the strategy and tactics of civil resistance. Widely translated, they have had an influence on the strategy of many resistance struggles.

Sharp's perspective differs from that of much of the pacifist movement, and indeed from his own earlier pacifist perspective, in that he acknowledges that war can play a role in the struggle to end oppression, deter aggression, and preserve free institutions. So the task, he argues, if we are to make the abolition of war a realistic goal, is to research and develop nonviolent alternatives; without them, governments will continue to be prepared to go to war. Similarly, without viable alternatives, people living under oppressive regimes or intolerable conditions will be prepared to resort to armed insurrection.

The power of nonviolent action stems from the fact that all governments, including dictatorial ones, depend on the co-operation, or at least the general compliance, of the people they govern, and in particular on the loyalty of key institutions - the army, the police, the civil service and, in the modern era, the media. If a government's base of support in society is eroded, it becomes increasingly difficult for it to govern, to the point where it can no longer rely on these crucial institutions of administration, persuasion and coercion. That insight is not new, and its validity has been demonstrated many times down the centuries, but increasingly so in the 20th and 21st centuries as the means of popular communication and mobilisation have expanded.

Sharp's particular contribution, in collaboration, to be sure, with colleagues and associates, has been to set out in a systematic way the elements involved in successful nonviolent action, to bring to light the historical evidence, and, in the context of insisting on the importance of advance planning and preparation, to identify the factors to be taken into account in devising sound strategies and tactics.

From Dictatorship to Democracy succinctly recapitulates the salient features of Sharp's approach in the situation where people are confronting dictatorial regimes. While those of us living in Western democracies do not face such extreme circumstances, the insights in this study are pertinent to campaigns against unjust and irresponsible policies in our own societies, as well as enabling us to understand and respond to the stirring events across the world which are reshaping global politics in the 21st century.

Michael Randle, March 2011

TABLE OF CONTENTS

PREFACE

One of my major concerns for many years has been how people could prevent and destroy dictatorships. This has been nurtured in part because of a belief that human beings should not be dominated and destroyed by such regimes. That belief has been strengthened by readings on the importance of human freedom, on the nature of dictatorships (from Aristotle to analysts of totalitarianism), and histories of dictatorships (especially the Nazi and Stalinist systems).

Over the years I have had occasion to get to know people who lived and suffered under Nazi rule, including some who survived concentration camps. In Norway I met people who had resisted fascist rule and survived, and heard of those who perished. I talked with Jews who had escaped the Nazi clutches and with persons who had helped to save them.

Knowledge of the terror of Communist rule in various countries has been learned more from books than personal contacts. The terror of these systems appeared to me to be especially poignant for these dictatorships were imposed in the name of liberation from oppression and exploitation.

In more recent decades through visits of persons from dictatorially ruled countries, such as Panama, Poland, Chile, Tibet, and Burma, the realities of today's dictatorships became more real. From Tibetans who had fought against Chinese Communist aggression, Russians who had defeated the August 1991 hard-line coup, and Thais who had nonviolently blocked a return to military rule, I have gained often troubling perspectives on the insidious nature of dictatorships.

The sense of pathos and outrage against the brutalities, along with admiration of the calm heroism of unbelievably brave men and women, were sometimes strengthened by visits to places where the dangers were still great, and yet defiance by brave people continued. These included Panama under Noriega; Vilnius, Lithuania, under continued Soviet repression; Tiananmen Square, Beijing, during both the festive demonstration of freedom and while the

first armored personnel carriers entered that fateful night; and the
jungle headquarters of the democratic opposition at Manerplaw in
"liberated Burma."

Sometimes I visited the sites of the fallen, as the television tower
and the cemetery in Vilnius, the public park in Riga where people
had been gunned down, the center of Ferrara in northern Italy where
the fascists lined up and shot resisters, and a simple cemetery in
Manerplaw filled with bodies of men who had died much too young.
It is a sad realization that every dictatorship leaves such death and
destruction in its wake.

Out of these concerns and experiences grew a determined
hope that prevention of tyranny might be possible, that successful
struggles against dictatorships could be waged without mass mu-
tual slaughters, that dictatorships could be destroyed and new ones
prevented from rising out of the ashes.

I have tried to think carefully about the most effective ways
in which dictatorships could be successfully disintegrated with the
least possible cost in suffering and lives. In this I have drawn on my
studies over many years of dictatorships, resistance movements,
revolutions, political thought, governmental systems, and especially
realistic nonviolent struggle.

This publication is the result. I am certain it is far from perfect.
But, perhaps, it offers some guidelines to assist thought and planning to produce movements of liberation that are more powerful
and effective than might otherwise be the case.

Of necessity, and of deliberate choice, the focus of this essay is
on the generic problem of how to destroy a dictatorship and to prevent the rise of a new one. I am not competent to produce a detailed
analysis and prescription for a particular country. However, it is my
hope that this generic analysis may be useful to people in, unfortunately, too many countries who now face the realities of dictatorial
rule. They will need to examine the validity of this analysis for their
situations and the extent to which its major recommendations are, or
can be made to be, applicable for their liberation struggles.

Nowhere in this analysis do I assume that defying dictators will
be an easy or cost-free endeavor. All forms of struggle have complica-

tions and costs. Fighting dictators will, of course, bring casualties. It is my hope, however, that this analysis will spur resistance leaders to consider strategies that may increase their effective power while reducing the relative level of casualties.

Nor should this analysis be interpreted to mean that when a specific dictatorship is ended, all other problems will also disappear. The fall of one regime does not bring in a utopia. Rather, it opens the way for hard work and long efforts to build more just social, economic, and political relationships and the eradication of other forms of injustices and oppression. It is my hope that this brief examination of how a dictatorship can be disintegrated may be found useful wherever people live under domination and desire to be free.

Gene Sharp

6 October 1993
Albert Einstein Institution
Boston, Massachusetts

ONE
FACING DICTATORSHIPS REALISTICALLY

In recent years various dictatorships — of both internal and external origin — have collapsed or stumbled when confronted by defiant, mobilized people. Often seen as firmly entrenched and impregnable, some of these dictatorships proved unable to withstand the concerted political, economic, and social defiance of the people.

Since 1980 dictatorships have collapsed before the predominantly nonviolent defiance of people in Estonia, Latvia, and Lithuania, Poland, East Germany, Czechoslovakia and Slovenia, Madagascar, Mali, Bolivia, and the Philippines. Nonviolent resistance has furthered the movement toward democratization in Nepal, Zambia, South Korea, Chile, Argentina, Haiti, Brazil, Uruguay, Malawi, Thailand, Bulgaria, Hungary, Nigeria, and various parts of the former Soviet Union (playing a significant role in the defeat of the August 1991 attempted hard-line coup d'état).

In addition, mass political defiance[1] has occurred in China, Burma, and Tibet in recent years. Although those struggles have not brought an end to the ruling dictatorships or occupations, they have exposed the brutal nature of those repressive regimes to the world community and have provided the populations with valuable experience with this form of struggle.

---

[1] The term used in this context was introduced by Robert Helvey. "Political defiance" is nonviolent struggle (protest, noncooperation, and intervention) applied defiantly and actively for political purposes. The term originated in response to the confusion and distortion created by equating nonviolent struggle with pacifism and moral or religious "nonviolence." "Defiance" denotes a deliberate challenge to authority by disobedience, allowing no room for submission. "Political defiance" describes the environment in which the action is employed (political) as well as the objective (political power). The term is used principally to describe action by populations to regain from dictatorships control over governmental institutions by relentlessly attacking their sources of power and deliberately using strategic planning and operations to do so. In this paper, political defiance, nonviolent resistance, and nonviolent struggle will be used interchangeably, although the latter two terms generally refer to struggles with a broader range of objectives (social, economic, psychological, etc.).

The collapse of dictatorships in the above named countries certainly has not erased all other problems in those societies: poverty, crime, bureaucratic inefficiency, and environmental destruction are often the legacy of brutal regimes. However, the downfall of these dictatorships has minimally lifted much of the suffering of the victims of oppression, and has opened the way for the rebuilding of these societies with greater political democracy, personal liberties, and social justice.

A continuing problem

There has indeed been a trend towards greater democratization and freedom in the world in the past decades. According to Freedom House, which compiles a yearly international survey of the status of political rights and civil liberties, the number of countries around the world classified as "Free" has grown significantly in recent years:[2]

	Free	Partly Free	Not Free
1983	54	47	64
1993	75	73	38
2003	89	55	48
2009	89	62	42

However, this positive trend is tempered by the large numbers of people still living under conditions of tyranny. As of 2008, 34% of the world's 6.68 billion population lived in countries designated as "Not Free,"[3] that is, areas with extremely restricted political rights and civil liberties. The 42 countries in the "Not Free" category are ruled by a range of military dictatorships (as in Burma), traditional repressive monarchies (as in Saudi Arabia and Bhutan), dominant political parties (as in China and North Korea), foreign occupiers (as in Tibet and Western Sahara), or are in a state of transition.

[2] Freedom House, *Freedom in the World*, http://www.freedomhouse.org.
[3] *Ibid.*

Many countries today are in a state of rapid economic, political, and social change. Although the number of "Free" countries has increased in recent years, there is a great risk that many nations, in the face of such rapid fundamental changes, will move in the opposite direction and experience new forms of dictatorship. Military cliques, ambitious individuals, elected officials, and doctrinal political parties will repeatedly seek to impose their will. Coups d'état are and will remain a common occurrence. Basic human and political rights will continue to be denied to vast numbers of peoples.

Unfortunately, the past is still with us. The problem of dictatorships is deep. People in many countries have experienced decades or even centuries of oppression, whether of domestic or foreign origin. Frequently, unquestioning submission to authority figures and rulers has been long inculcated. In extreme cases, the social, political, economic, and even religious institutions of the society — outside of state control — have been deliberately weakened, subordinated, or even replaced by new regimented institutions used by the state or ruling party to control the society. The population has often been atomized (turned into a mass of isolated individuals) unable to work together to achieve freedom, to confide in each other, or even to do much of anything at their own initiative.

The result is predictable: the population becomes weak, lacks self-confidence, and is incapable of resistance. People are often too frightened to share their hatred of the dictatorship and their hunger for freedom even with family and friends. People are often too terrified to think seriously of public resistance. In any case, what would be the use? Instead, they face suffering without purpose and a future without hope.

Current conditions in today's dictatorships may be much worse than earlier. In the past, some people may have attempted resistance. Short-lived mass protests and demonstrations may have occurred. Perhaps spirits soared temporarily. At other times, individuals and small groups may have conducted brave but impotent gestures, asserting some principle or simply their defiance. However noble the motives, such past acts of resistance have often been insufficient to overcome the people's fear and habit of obedience, a necessary prerequisite to destroy the dictatorship. Sadly, those acts may have brought instead only increased suffering and death, not victories or even hope.

Freedom through violence?

What is to be done in such circumstances? The obvious possibilities seem useless. Constitutional and legal barriers, judicial decisions, and public opinion are normally ignored by dictators. Understandably, reacting to the brutalities, torture, disappearances, and killings, people often have concluded that only violence can end a dictatorship. Angry victims have sometimes organized to fight the brutal dictators with whatever violent and military capacity they could muster, despite the odds being against them. These people have often fought bravely, at great cost in suffering and lives. Their accomplishments have sometimes been remarkable, but they rarely have won freedom. Violent rebellions can trigger brutal repression that frequently leaves the populace more helpless than before.

Whatever the merits of the violent option, however, one point is clear. *By placing confidence in violent means, one has chosen the very type of struggle with which the oppressors nearly always have superiority.* The dictators are equipped to apply violence overwhelmingly. However long or briefly these democrats can continue, eventually the harsh military realities usually become inescapable. The dictators almost always have superiority in military hardware, ammunition, transportation, and the size of military forces. Despite bravery, the democrats are (almost always) no match.

When conventional military rebellion is recognized as unrealistic, some dissidents then favor guerrilla warfare. However, guerrilla warfare rarely, if ever, benefits the oppressed population or ushers in a democracy. Guerrilla warfare is no obvious solution, particularly given the very strong tendency toward immense casualties among one's own people. The technique is no guarantor against failure, despite supporting theory and strategic analyses, and sometimes international backing. Guerrilla struggles often last a very long time. Civilian populations are often displaced by the ruling government, with immense human suffering and social dislocation.

Even when successful, guerrilla struggles often have significant long-term negative structural consequences. Immediately, the
attacked regime becomes more dictatorial as a result of its coun-
termeasures. If the guerrillas should finally succeed, the resulting
new regime is often more dictatorial than its predecessor due to the
centralizing impact of the expanded military forces and the weakening or destruction of the society's independent groups and institutions during the struggle — bodies that are vital in establishing and
maintaining a democratic society. Persons hostile to dictatorships
should look for another option.

Coups, elections, foreign saviors?

A military coup d'état against a dictatorship might appear to be
relatively one of the easiest and quickest ways to remove a particularly repugnant regime. However, there are very serious problems
with that technique. Most importantly, it leaves in place the existing
maldistribution of power between the population and the elite in
control of the government and its military forces. The removal of
particular persons and cliques from the governing positions most
likely will merely make it possible for another group to take their
place. Theoretically, this group might be milder in its behavior and
be open in limited ways to democratic reforms. However, the opposite is as likely to be the case.

After consolidating its position, the new clique may turn out to
be more ruthless and more ambitious than the old one. Consequently,
the new clique — in which hopes may have been placed — will be
able to do whatever it wants without concern for democracy or
human rights. That is not an acceptable answer to the problem of
dictatorship.

Elections are not available under dictatorships as an instrument of significant political change. Some dictatorial regimes,
such as those of the former Soviet-dominated Eastern bloc, went
through the motions in order to appear democratic. Those elections,
however, were merely rigidly controlled plebiscites to get public

endorsement of candidates already hand picked by the dictators. Dictators under pressure may at times agree to new elections, but then rig them to place civilian puppets in government offices. If opposition candidates have been allowed to run and were actually elected, as occurred in Burma in 1990 and Nigeria in 1993, results may simply be ignored and the "victors" subjected to intimidation, arrest, or even execution. Dictators are not in the business of allowing elections that could remove them from their thrones.

Many people now suffering under a brutal dictatorship, or who have gone into exile to escape its immediate grasp, do not believe that the oppressed can liberate themselves. They expect that their people can only be saved by the actions of others. These people place their confidence in external forces. They believe that only international help can be strong enough to bring down the dictators.

The view that the oppressed are unable to act effectively is sometimes accurate for a certain time period. As noted, often oppressed people are unwilling and temporarily unable to struggle because they have no confidence in their ability to face the ruthless dictatorship, and no known way to save themselves. It is therefore understandable that many people place their hope for liberation in others. This outside force may be "public opinion," the United Nations, a particular country, or international economic and political sanctions.

Such a scenario may sound comforting, but there are grave problems with this reliance on an outside savior. Such confidence may be totally misplaced. Usually no foreign saviors are coming, and if a foreign state does intervene, it probably should not be trusted.

A few harsh realities concerning reliance on foreign intervention need to be emphasized here:

- Frequently foreign states will tolerate, or even positively assist, a dictatorship in order to advance their own economic or political interests.

- Foreign states also may be willing to sell out an oppressed people instead of keeping pledges to assist their liberation at the cost of another objective.

- Some foreign states will act against a dictatorship only to gain their own economic, political, or military control over the country.

- The foreign states may become actively involved for positive purposes only if and when the internal resistance movement has already begun shaking the dictatorship, having thereby focused international attention on the brutal nature of the regime.

Dictatorships usually exist primarily because of the internal power distribution in the home country. The population and society are too weak to cause the dictatorship serious problems, wealth and power are concentrated in too few hands. Although dictatorships may benefit from or be somewhat weakened by international actions, their continuation is dependent primarily on internal factors.

International pressures can be very useful, however, when they are supporting a powerful internal resistance movement. Then, for example, international economic boycotts, embargoes, the breaking of diplomatic relations, expulsion from international organizations, condemnation by United Nations bodies, and the like can assist greatly. However, in the absence of a strong internal resistance movement such actions by others are unlikely to happen.

Facing the hard truth

The conclusion is a hard one. When one wants to bring down a dictatorship most effectively and with the least cost then one has four immediate tasks:

- One must strengthen the oppressed population themselves in their determination, self-confidence, and resistance skills;

- One must strengthen the independent social groups and institutions of the oppressed people;

- One must create a powerful internal resistance force; and

- One must develop a wise grand strategic plan for liberation and implement it skillfully.

A liberation struggle is a time for self-reliance and internal strengthening of the struggle group. As Charles Stewart Parnell called out during the Irish rent strike campaign in 1879 and 1880:

> It is no use relying on the Government . . . . You must only rely upon your own determination . . . . [H]elp yourselves by standing together . . . strengthen those amongst yourselves who are weak . . . , band yourselves together, organize yourselves . . . and you must win . . .

> When you have made this question ripe for settlement, then and not till then will it be settled.[4]

Against a strong self-reliant force, given wise strategy, disciplined and courageous action, and genuine strength, the dictatorship will eventually crumble. Minimally, however, the above four requirements must be fulfilled.

As the above discussion indicates, liberation from dictatorships ultimately depends on the people's ability to liberate themselves. The cases of successful political defiance — or nonviolent struggle for political ends — cited above indicate that the means do exist for populations to free themselves, but that option has remained undeveloped. We will examine this option in detail in the following chapters. However, we should first look at the issue of negotiations as a means of dismantling dictatorships.

---

[4] Patrick Sarsfield O'Hegarty, *A History of Ireland Under the Union, 1880-1922* (London: Methuen, 1952), pp. 490-491.

TWO
THE DANGERS OF NEGOTIATIONS

When faced with the severe problems of confronting a dictatorship (as surveyed in Chapter One), some people may lapse back into passive submission. Others, seeing no prospect of achieving democracy, may conclude they must come to terms with the apparently permanent dictatorship, hoping that through "conciliation," "compromise," and "negotiations" they might be able to salvage some positive elements and to end the brutalities. On the surface, lacking realistic options, there is appeal in that line of thinking.

Serious struggle against brutal dictatorships is not a pleasant prospect. Why is it necessary to go that route? Can't everyone just be reasonable and find ways to talk, to negotiate the way to a gradual end to the dictatorship? Can't the democrats appeal to the dictators' sense of common humanity and convince them to reduce their domination bit by bit, and perhaps finally to give way completely to the establishment of a democracy?

It is sometimes argued that the truth is not all on one side. Perhaps the democrats have misunderstood the dictators, who may have acted from good motives in difficult circumstances? Or perhaps some may think, the dictators would gladly remove themselves from the difficult situation facing the country if only given some encouragement and enticements. It may be argued that the dictators could be offered a "win-win" solution, in which everyone gains something. The risks and pain of further struggle could be unnecessary, it may be argued, if the democratic opposition is only willing to settle the conflict peacefully by negotiations (which may even perhaps be assisted by some skilled individuals or even another government). Would that not be preferable to a difficult struggle, even if it is one conducted by nonviolent struggle rather than by military war?

Merits and limitations of negotiations

Negotiations are a very useful tool in resolving certain types of issues in conflicts and should not be neglected or rejected when they
are appropriate.

In some situations where no fundamental issues are at stake,
and therefore a compromise is acceptable, negotiations can be an
important means to settle a conflict. A labor strike for higher wages
is a good example of the appropriate role of negotiations in a conflict:
a negotiated settlement may provide an increase somewhere between
the sums originally proposed by each of the contending sides. Labor
conflicts with legal trade unions are, however, quite different than
the conflicts in which the continued existence of a cruel dictatorship
or the establishment of political freedom are at stake.

When the issues at stake are fundamental, affecting religious
principles, issues of human freedom, or the whole future development of the society, negotiations do not provide a way of reaching a
mutually satisfactory solution. On some basic issues there should
be no compromise. Only a shift in power relations in favor of the
democrats can adequately safeguard the basic issues at stake. Such
a shift will occur through struggle, not negotiations. This is not to
say that negotiations ought never to be used. The point here is that
negotiations are not a realistic way to remove a strong dictatorship
in the absence of a powerful democratic opposition.

Negotiations, of course, may not be an option at all. Firmly
entrenched dictators who feel secure in their position may refuse to
negotiate with their democratic opponents. Or, when negotiations
have been initiated, the democratic negotiators may disappear and
never be heard from again.

Negotiated surrender?

Individuals and groups who oppose dictatorship and favor negotiations will often have good motives. Especially when a military
struggle has continued for years against a brutal dictatorship without
final victory, it is understandable that all the people of whatever

political persuasion would want peace. Negotiations are especially likely to become an issue among democrats where the dictators have clear military superiority and the destruction and casualties among one's own people are no longer bearable. There will then be a strong temptation to explore any other route that might salvage some of the democrats' objectives while bringing an end to the cycle of violence and counter-violence.

The offer by a dictatorship of "peace" through negotiations with the democratic opposition is, of course, rather disingenuous. The violence could be ended immediately by the dictators themselves, if only they would stop waging war on their own people. They could at their own initiative without any bargaining restore respect for human dignity and rights, free political prisoners, end torture, halt military operations, withdraw from the government, and apologize to the people.

When the dictatorship is strong but an irritating resistance exists, the dictators may wish to negotiate the opposition into surrender under the guise of making "peace." The call to negotiate can sound appealing, but grave dangers can be lurking within the negotiating room.

On the other hand, when the opposition is exceptionally strong and the dictatorship is genuinely threatened, the dictators may seek negotiations in order to salvage as much of their control or wealth as possible. In neither case should the democrats help the dictators achieve their goals.

Democrats should be wary of the traps that may be deliberately built into a negotiation process by the dictators. The call for negotiations when basic issues of political liberties are involved may be an effort by the dictators to induce the democrats to surrender peacefully while the violence of the dictatorship continues. In those types of conflicts the only proper role of negotiations may occur at the end of a decisive struggle in which the power of the dictators has been effectively destroyed and they seek personal safe passage to an international airport.

Power and justice in negotiations

If this judgment sounds too harsh a commentary on negotiations, perhaps some of the romanticism associated with them needs to be moderated. Clear thinking is required as to how negotiations operate.

"Negotiation" does not mean that the two sides sit down together on a basis of equality and talk through and resolve the differences that produced the conflict between them. Two facts must be remembered. First, in negotiations it is not the relative justice of the conflicting views and objectives that determines the content of a negotiated agreement. Second, the content of a negotiated agreement is largely determined by the power capacity of each side.

Several difficult questions must be considered. What can each side do at a later date to gain its objectives if the other side fails to come to an agreement at the negotiating table? What can each side do after an agreement is reached if the other side breaks its word and uses its available forces to seize its objectives despite the agreement?

A settlement is not reached in negotiations through an assessment of the rights and wrongs of the issues at stake. While those may be much discussed, the real results in negotiations come from an assessment of the absolute and relative power situations of the contending groups. What can the democrats do to ensure that their minimum claims cannot be denied? What can the dictators do to stay in control and neutralize the democrats? In other words, if an agreement comes, it is more likely the result of each side estimating how the power capacities of the two sides compare, and then calculating how an open struggle might end.

Attention must also be given to what each side is willing to give up in order to reach agreement. In successful negotiations there is compromise, a splitting of differences. Each side gets part of what it wants and gives up part of its objectives.

In the case of extreme dictatorships what are the pro-democracy forces to give up to the dictators? What objectives of the dictators are the pro-democracy forces to accept? Are the democrats to give to the dictators (whether a political party or a military cabal) a constitutionally-established permanent role in the future government? Where is the democracy in that?

Even assuming that all goes well in negotiations, it is necessary to ask: What kind of peace will be the result? Will life then be better or worse than it would be if the democrats began or continued to struggle?

"Agreeable" dictators

Dictators may have a variety of motives and objectives underlying their domination: power, position, wealth, reshaping the society, and the like. One should remember that none of these will be served if they abandon their control positions. In the event of negotiations dictators will try to preserve their goals.

Whatever promises offered by dictators in any negotiated settlement, no one should ever forget that the dictators may promise anything to secure submission from their democratic opponents, and then brazenly violate those same agreements.

If the democrats agree to halt resistance in order to gain a reprieve from repression, they may be very disappointed. A halt to resistance rarely brings reduced repression. Once the restraining force of internal and international opposition has been removed, dictators may even make their oppression and violence more brutal than before. The collapse of popular resistance often removes the countervailing force that has limited the control and brutality of the dictatorship. The tyrants can then move ahead against whomever they wish. "For the tyrant has the power to inflict only that which we lack the strength to resist," wrote Krishnalal Shridharani.[5]

Resistance, not negotiations, is essential for change in conflicts where fundamental issues are at stake. In nearly all cases, resistance must continue to drive dictators out of power. Success is most often

---

[5] Krishnalal Shridharani, *War Without Violence: A Study of Gandhi's Method and Its Accomplishments* (New York: Harcourt, Brace, 1939, and reprint New York and London: Garland Publishing, 1972), p. 260.

determined not by negotiating a settlement but through the wise use of the most appropriate and powerful means of resistance available. It is our contention, to be explored later in more detail, that political defiance, or nonviolent struggle, is the most powerful means available to those struggling for freedom.

What kind of peace?

If dictators and democrats are to talk about peace at all, extremely clear thinking is needed because of the dangers involved. Not everyone who uses the word "peace" wants peace with freedom and justice. Submission to cruel oppression and passive acquiescence to ruthless dictators who have perpetrated atrocities on hundreds of thousands of people is no real peace. Hitler often called for peace, by which he meant submission to his will. A dictators' peace is often no more than the peace of the prison or of the grave.

There are other dangers. Well-intended negotiators sometimes confuse the objectives of the negotiations and the negotiation process itself. Further, democratic negotiators, or foreign negotiation specialists accepted to assist in the negotiations, may in a single stroke provide the dictators with the domestic and international legitimacy that they had been previously denied because of their seizure of the state, human rights violations, and brutalities. Without that desperately needed legitimacy, the dictators cannot continue to rule indefinitely. Exponents of peace should not provide them legitimacy.

Reasons for hope

As stated earlier, opposition leaders may feel forced to pursue negotiations out of a sense of hopelessness of the democratic struggle. However, that sense of powerlessness can be changed. Dictatorships are not permanent. People living under dictatorships need not remain weak, and dictators need not be allowed to remain powerful indefinitely. Aristotle noted long ago, ". . . [O]ligarchy and tyranny are shorter-lived than any other constitution. . . . [A]ll round, tyrannies have not lasted long."[6] Modern dictatorships are also vulnerable. Their weaknesses can be aggravated and the dictators' power can be disintegrated. (In Chapter Four we will examine these weaknesses in more detail.)

Recent history shows the vulnerability of dictatorships, and reveals that they can crumble in a relatively short time span: whereas ten years — 1980-1990 — were required to bring down the Communist dictatorship in Poland, in East Germany and Czechoslovakia in 1989 it occurred within weeks. In El Salvador and Guatemala in 1944 the struggles against the entrenched brutal military dictators required approximately two weeks each. The militarily powerful regime of the Shah in Iran was undermined in a few months. The Marcos dictatorship in the Philippines fell before people power within weeks in 1986: the United States government quickly abandoned President Marcos when the strength of the opposition became apparent. The attempted hard-line coup in the Soviet Union in August 1991 was blocked in days by political defiance. Thereafter, many of its long dominated constituent nations in only days, weeks, and months regained their independence.

The old preconception that violent means always work quickly and nonviolent means always require vast time is clearly not valid. Although much time may be required for changes in the underlying situation and society, the actual fight against a dictatorship sometimes occurs relatively quickly by nonviolent struggle.

Negotiations are not the only alternative to a continuing war of annihilation on the one hand and capitulation on the other. The examples just cited, as well as those listed in Chapter One, illustrate that another option exists for those who want both peace *and* freedom: political defiance.

---

[6] Aristotle, *The Politics*, transl. by T. A. Sinclair (Harmondsworth, Middlesex, England and Baltimore, Maryland: Penguin Books 1976 [1962]), Book V, Chapter 12, pp. 231 and 232.

THREE
WHENCE COMES THE POWER?

Achieving a society with both freedom and peace is of course no simple task. It will require great strategic skill, organization, and planning. Above all, it will require power. Democrats cannot hope to bring down a dictatorship and establish political freedom without the ability to apply their own power effectively.

But how is this possible? What kind of power can the democratic opposition mobilize that will be sufficient to destroy the dictatorship and its vast military and police networks? The answers lie in an oft ignored understanding of political power. Learning this insight is not really so difficult a task. Some basic truths are quite simple.

The "Monkey Master" fable

A Fourteenth Century Chinese parable by Liu-Ji, for example, outlines this neglected understanding of political power quite well:[7]

> In the feudal state of Chu an old man survived by keeping monkeys in his service. The people of Chu called him "ju gong" (monkey master).
>
> Each morning, the old man would assemble the monkeys in his courtyard, and order the eldest one to lead the others to the mountains to gather fruits from bushes and trees. It was the rule that each monkey had to give one-tenth of his collection to the old man. Those who failed to do so would be ruthlessly flogged. All the monkeys suffered bitterly, but dared not complain.

---

[7] This story, originally titled "Rule by Tricks" is from *Yu-li-zi* by Liu Ji (1311-1375) and has been translated by Sidney Tai, all rights reserved. Yu-li-zi is also the pseudonym of Liu Ji. The translation was originally published in *Nonviolent Sanctions: News from the Albert Einstein Institution* (Cambridge, Mass.), Vol. IV, No. 3 (Winter 1992-1993), p. 3.

One day, a small monkey asked the other monkeys: "Did the old man plant all the fruit trees and bushes?" The others said: "No, they grew naturally." The small monkey further asked: "Can't we take the fruits without the old man's permission?" The others replied: "Yes, we all can." The small monkey continued: "Then, why should we depend on the old man; why must we all serve him?"

Before the small monkey was able to finish his statement, all the monkeys suddenly became enlightened and awakened.

On the same night, watching that the old man had fallen asleep, the monkeys tore down all the barricades of the stockade in which they were confined, and destroyed the stockade entirely. They also took the fruits the old man had in storage, brought all with them to the woods, and never returned. The old man finally died of starvation.

Yu-li-zi says, "Some men in the world rule their people by tricks and not by righteous principles. Aren't they just like the monkey master? They are not aware of their muddle-headedness. As soon as their people become enlightened, their tricks no longer work."

Necessary sources of political power

The principle is simple. Dictators require the assistance of the people they rule, without which they cannot secure and maintain the sources of political power. These sources of political power include:

- *Authority*, the belief among the people that the regime is legitimate, and that they have a moral duty to obey it;

- *Human resources*, the number and importance of the persons and groups which are obeying, cooperating, or providing assistance to the rulers;

- *Skills and knowledge,* needed by the regime to perform specific actions and supplied by the cooperating persons and groups;

- *Intangible factors,* psychological and ideological factors that may induce people to obey and assist the rulers;

- *Material resources,* the degree to which the rulers control or have access to property, natural resources, financial resources, the economic system, and means of communication and transportation; and

- *Sanctions,* punishments, threatened or applied, against the disobedient and noncooperative to ensure the submission and cooperation that are needed for the regime to exist and carry out its policies.

All of these sources, however, depend on acceptance of the regime, on the submission and obedience of the population, and on the cooperation of innumerable people and the many institutions of the society. These are not guaranteed.

Full cooperation, obedience, and support will increase the availability of the needed sources of power and, consequently, expand the power capacity of any government.

On the other hand, withdrawal of popular and institutional cooperation with aggressors and dictators diminishes, and may sever, the availability of the sources of power on which all rulers depend. Without availability of those sources, the rulers' power weakens and finally dissolves.

Naturally, dictators are sensitive to actions and ideas that threaten their capacity to do as they like. Dictators are therefore likely to threaten and punish those who disobey, strike, or fail to cooperate. However, that is not the end of the story. Repression, even brutalities, do not always produce a resumption of the necessary degree of submission and cooperation for the regime to function.

If, despite repression, the sources of power can be restricted or severed for enough time, the initial results may be uncertainty and confusion within the dictatorship. That is likely to be followed by a clear weakening of the power of the dictatorship. Over time, the withholding of the sources of power can produce the paralysis and impotence of the regime, and in severe cases, its disintegration. The dictators' power will die, slowly or rapidly, from political starvation.

The degree of liberty or tyranny in any government is, it follows, in large degree a reflection of the relative determination of the subjects to be free and their willingness and ability to resist efforts to enslave them.

Contrary to popular opinion, even totalitarian dictatorships are dependent on the population and the societies they rule. As the political scientist Karl W. Deutsch noted in 1953:

> Totalitarian power is strong only if it does not have to be used too often. If totalitarian power must be used at all times against the entire population, it is unlikely to remain powerful for long. Since totalitarian regimes require more power for dealing with their subjects than do other types of government, such regimes stand in greater need of widespread and dependable compliance habits among their people; more than that they have to be able to count on the active support of at least significant parts of the population in case of need.[8]

The English Nineteenth Century legal theorist John Austin described the situation of a dictatorship confronting a disaffected people. Austin argued that if most of the population were determined to destroy the government and were willing to endure repression to do so, then the might of the government, including those who supported it, could not preserve the hated government, even if

---

[8] Karl W. Deutsch, "Cracks in the Monolith," in Carl J. Friedrich, ed., *Totalitarianism* (Cambridge, Mass.: Harvard University Press, 1954), pp. 313-314.

it received foreign assistance. The defiant people could not be forced back into permanent obedience and subjection, Austin concluded.[9]

Niccolo Machiavelli had much earlier argued that the prince ". . . who has the public as a whole for his enemy can never make himself secure; and the greater his cruelty, the weaker does his regime become."[10]

The practical political application of these insights was demonstrated by the heroic Norwegian resisters against the Nazi occupation, and as cited in Chapter One, by the brave Poles, Germans, Czechs, Slovaks, and many others who resisted Communist aggression and dictatorship, and finally helped produce the collapse of Communist rule in Europe. This, of course, is no new phenomenon: cases of nonviolent resistance go back at least to 494 B.C. when plebeians withdrew cooperation from their Roman patrician masters.[11] Nonviolent struggle has been employed at various times by peoples throughout Asia, Africa, the Americas, Australasia, and the Pacific islands, as well as Europe.

Three of the most important factors in determining to what degree a government's power will be controlled or uncontrolled therefore are: (1) the relative *desire* of the populace to impose limits on the government's power; (2) the relative *strength* of the subjects' independent organizations and institutions to withdraw collectively the sources of power; and (3) the population's relative *ability* to withhold their consent and assistance.

Centers of democratic power

One characteristic of a democratic society is that there exist independent of the state a multitude of nongovernmental groups and

---

[9] John Austin, *Lectures on Jurisprudence or the Philosophy of Positive Law* (Fifth edition, revised and edited by Robert Campbell, 2 vol., London: John Murray, 1911 [1861]), Vol. I, p. 296.

[10] Niccolo Machiavelli, "The Discourses on the First Ten Books of Livy," in *The Discourses of Niccolo Machiavelli* (London: Routledge and Kegan Paul, 1950), Vol. I, p. 254.

[11] See Gene Sharp, *The Politics of Nonviolent Action* (Boston: Porter Sargent, 1973), p. 75 and passim for other historical examples.

institutions. These include, for example, families, religious organizations, cultural associations, sports clubs, economic institutions, trade unions, student associations, political parties, villages, neighborhood associations, gardening clubs, human rights organizations, musical groups, literary societies, and others. These bodies are important in serving their own objectives and also in helping to meet social needs.

Additionally, these bodies have great political significance. They provide group and institutional bases by which people can exert influence over the direction of their society and resist other groups or the government when they are seen to impinge unjustly on their interests, activities, or purposes. Isolated individuals, not members of such groups, usually are unable to make a significant impact on the rest of the society, much less a government, and certainly not a dictatorship.

Consequently, if the autonomy and freedom of such bodies can be taken away by the dictators, the population will be relatively helpless. Also, if these institutions can themselves be dictatorially controlled by the central regime or replaced by new controlled ones, they can be used to dominate both the individual members and also those areas of the society.

However, if the autonomy and freedom of these independent civil institutions (outside of government control) can be maintained or regained they are highly important for the application of political defiance. The common feature of the cited examples in which dictatorships have been disintegrated or weakened has been the courageous *mass* application of political defiance by the population and its institutions.

As stated, these centers of power provide the institutional bases from which the population can exert pressure or can resist dictatorial controls. In the future, they will be part of the indispensable structural base for a free society. Their continued independence and growth therefore is often a prerequisite for the success of the liberation struggle.

If the dictatorship has been largely successful in destroying or controlling the society's independent bodies, it will be important for the resisters to create new independent social groups and institutions, or to reassert democratic control over surviving or partially controlled bodies. During the Hungarian Revolution of 1956-1957 a multitude of direct democracy councils emerged, even joining together to establish for some weeks a whole federated system of institutions and governance. In Poland during the late 1980s workers maintained illegal Solidarity unions and, in some cases, took over control of the official, Communist-dominated, trade unions. Such institutional developments can have very important political consequences.

Of course, none of this means that weakening and destroying dictatorships is easy, nor that every attempt will succeed. It certainly does not mean that the struggle will be free of casualties, for those still serving the dictators are likely to fight back in an effort to force the populace to resume cooperation and obedience.

The above insight into power does mean, however, that the deliberate disintegration of dictatorships is possible. Dictatorships in particular have specific characteristics that render them highly vulnerable to skillfully implemented political defiance. Let us examine these characteristics in more detail.

FOUR
DICTATORSHIPS HAVE WEAKNESSES

Dictatorships often appear invulnerable. Intelligence agencies, police, military forces, prisons, concentration camps, and execution squads are controlled by a powerful few. A country's finances, natural resources, and production capacities are often arbitrarily plundered by dictators and used to support the dictators' will.

In comparison, democratic opposition forces often appear extremely weak, ineffective, and powerless. That perception of invulnerability against powerlessness makes effective opposition unlikely.

That is not the whole story, however.

Identifying the Achilles' heel

A myth from Classical Greece illustrates well the vulnerability of the supposedly invulnerable. Against the warrior Achilles, no blow would injure and no sword would penetrate his skin. When still a baby, Achilles' mother had supposedly dipped him into the waters of the magical river Styx, resulting in the protection of his body from all dangers. There was, however, a problem. Since the baby was held by his heel so that he would not be washed away, the magical water had not covered that small part of his body. When Achilles was a grown man he appeared to all to be invulnerable to the enemies' weapons. However, in the battle against Troy, instructed by one who knew the weakness, an enemy soldier aimed his arrow at Achilles' unprotected heel, the one spot where he could be injured. The strike proved fatal. Still today, the phrase "Achilles' heel" refers to the vulnerable part of a person, a plan, or an institution at which if attacked there is no protection.

The same principle applies to ruthless dictatorships. They, too, can be conquered, but most quickly and with least cost if their weaknesses can be identified and the attack concentrated on them.

Weaknesses of dictatorships

Among the weaknesses of dictatorships are the following:

1. The cooperation of a multitude of people, groups, and institutions needed to operate the system may be restricted or withdrawn.

2. The requirements and effects of the regime's past policies will somewhat limit its present ability to adopt and implement conflicting policies.

3. The system may become routine in its operation, less able to adjust quickly to new situations.

4. Personnel and resources already allocated for existing tasks will not be easily available for new needs.

5. Subordinates fearful of displeasing their superiors may not report accurate or complete information needed by the dictators to make decisions.

6. The ideology may erode, and myths and symbols of the system may become unstable.

7. If a strong ideology is present that influences one's view of reality, firm adherence to it may cause inattention to actual conditions and needs.

8. Deteriorating efficiency and competency of the bureaucracy, or excessive controls and regulations, may make the system's policies and operation ineffective.

9. Internal institutional conflicts and personal rivalries and hostilities may harm, and even disrupt, the operation of the dictatorship.

10. Intellectuals and students may become restless in response to conditions, restrictions, doctrinalism, and repression.

11. The general public may over time become apathetic, skeptical, and even hostile to the regime.

12. Regional, class, cultural, or national differences may become acute.

13. The power hierarchy of the dictatorship is always unstable to some degree, and at times extremely so. Individuals do not only remain in the same position in the ranking, but may rise or fall to other ranks or be removed entirely and replaced by new persons.

14. Sections of the police or military forces may act to achieve their own objectives, even against the will of established dictators, including by coup d'état.

15. If the dictatorship is new, time is required for it to become well established.

16. With so many decisions made by so few people in the dictatorship, mistakes of judgment, policy, and action are likely to occur.

17. If the regime seeks to avoid these dangers and decentralizes controls and decision making, its control over the central levers of power may be further eroded.

Attacking weaknesses of dictatorships

With knowledge of such inherent weaknesses, the democratic opposition can seek to aggravate these "Achilles' heels" deliberately in order to alter the system drastically or to disintegrate it.

The conclusion is then clear: despite the appearances of strength, all dictatorships have weaknesses, internal inefficiencies, personal rivalries, institutional inefficiencies, and conflicts between organizations and departments. These weaknesses, over time, tend to make the regime less effective and more vulnerable to changing conditions and deliberate resistance. Not everything the regime sets out to accomplish will get completed. At times, for example, even Hitler's direct orders were never implemented because those beneath him in the hierarchy refused to carry them out. The dictatorial regime may at times even fall apart quickly, as we have already observed.

This does not mean dictatorships can be destroyed without risks and casualties. Every possible course of action for liberation will involve risks and potential suffering, and will take time to operate. And, of course, no means of action can ensure rapid success in every situation. However, types of struggle that target the dictatorship's identifiable weaknesses have greater chance of success than those that seek to fight the dictatorship where it is clearly strongest. The question is *how* this struggle is to be waged.

FIVE
EXERCISING POWER

In Chapter One we noted that military resistance against dictatorships does not strike them where they are weakest, but rather where they are strongest. By choosing to compete in the areas of military forces, supplies of ammunition, weapons technology, and the like, resistance movements tend to put themselves at a distinct disadvantage. Dictatorships will almost always be able to muster superior resources in these areas. The dangers of relying on foreign powers for salvation were also outlined. In Chapter Two we examined the problems of relying on negotiations as a means to remove dictatorships.

What means are then available that will offer the democratic resistance distinct advantages and will tend to aggravate the identified weaknesses of dictatorships? What technique of action will capitalize on the theory of political power discussed in Chapter Three? The alternative of choice is political defiance.

Political defiance has the following characteristics:

- It does not accept that the outcome will be decided by the means of fighting chosen by the dictatorship.

- It is difficult for the regime to combat.

- It can uniquely aggravate weaknesses of the dictatorship and can sever its sources of power.

- It can in action be widely dispersed but can also be concentrated on a specific objective.

- It leads to errors of judgment and action by the dictators.

- It can effectively utilize the population as a whole and the society's groups and institutions in the struggle to end the brutal domination of the few.

- It helps to spread the distribution of effective power in the society, making the establishment and maintenance of a democratic society more possible.

The workings of nonviolent struggle

Like military capabilities, political defiance can be employed for a variety of purposes, ranging from efforts to influence the opponents to take different actions, to create conditions for a peaceful resolution of conflict, or to disintegrate the opponents' regime. However, political defiance operates in quite different ways from violence. Although both techniques are means to wage struggle, they do so with very different means and with different consequences. The ways and results of violent conflict are well known. Physical weapons are used to intimidate, injure, kill, and destroy.

Nonviolent struggle is a much more complex and varied means of struggle than is violence. Instead, the struggle is fought by psychological, social, economic, and political weapons applied by the population and the institutions of the society. These have been known under various names of protests, strikes, noncooperation, boycotts, disaffection, and people power. As noted earlier, all governments can rule only as long as they receive replenishment of the needed sources of their power from the cooperation, submission, and obedience of the population and the institutions of the society. Political defiance, unlike violence, is uniquely suited to severing those sources of power.

Nonviolent weapons and discipline

The common error of past improvised political defiance campaigns is the reliance on only one or two methods, such as strikes and mass demonstrations. In fact, a multitude of methods exist that allow resistance strategists to concentrate and disperse resistance as required.

About two hundred specific methods of nonviolent action have been identified, and there are certainly scores more. These methods are classified under three broad categories: protest and persuasion, noncooperation, and intervention. Methods of nonviolent protest and persuasion are largely symbolic demonstrations, including parades, marches, and vigils (54 methods). Noncooperation is divided into three sub-categories: (a) social noncooperation (16 methods), (b) economic noncooperation, including boycotts (26 methods) and strikes (23 methods), and (c) political noncooperation (38 methods). Nonviolent intervention, by psychological, physical, social, economic, or political means, such as the fast, nonviolent occupation, and parallel government (41 methods), is the final group. A list of 198 of these methods is included as the Appendix to this publication.

The use of a considerable number of these methods — carefully chosen, applied persistently and on a large scale, wielded in the context of a wise strategy and appropriate tactics, by trained civilians — is likely to cause any illegitimate regime severe problems. This applies to all dictatorships.

In contrast to military means, the methods of nonviolent struggle can be focused directly on the issues at stake. For example, since the issue of dictatorship is primarily political, then political forms of nonviolent struggle would be crucial. These would include denial of legitimacy to the dictators and noncooperation with their regime. Noncooperation would also be applied against specific policies. At times stalling and procrastination may be quietly and even secretly practiced, while at other times open disobedience and defiant public demonstrations and strikes may be visible to all.

On the other hand, if the dictatorship is vulnerable to economic pressures or if many of the popular grievances against it are economic, then economic action, such as boycotts or strikes, may be appropriate resistance methods. The dictators' efforts to exploit the economic system might be met with limited general strikes, slowdowns, and refusal of assistance by (or disappearance of) indispensable experts. Selective use of various types of strikes may be conducted at key points in manufacturing, in transport, in the supply of raw materials, and in the distribution of products.

Some methods of nonviolent struggle require people to perform acts unrelated to their normal lives, such as distributing leaflets, operating an underground press, going on hunger strike, or sitting down in the streets. These methods may be difficult for some people to undertake except in very extreme situations.

Other methods of nonviolent struggle instead require people to continue approximately their normal lives, though in somewhat different ways. For example, people may report for work, instead of striking, but then deliberately work more slowly or inefficiently than usual. "Mistakes" may be consciously made more frequently. One may become "sick" and "unable" to work at certain times. Or, one may simply refuse to work. One might go to religious services when the act expresses not only religious but also political convictions. One may act to protect children from the attackers' propaganda by education at home or in illegal classes. One might refuse to join certain "recommended" or required organizations that one would not have joined freely in earlier times. The similarity of such types of action to people's usual activities and the limited degree of departure from their normal lives may make participation in the national liberation struggle much easier for many people.

Since nonviolent struggle and violence operate in fundamentally different ways, even limited resistance violence during a political defiance campaign will be counterproductive, for it will shift the struggle to one in which the dictators have an overwhelming advantage (military warfare). Nonviolent discipline is a key to success and must be maintained despite provocations and brutalities by the dictators and their agents.

The maintenance of nonviolent discipline against violent opponents facilitates the workings of the four mechanisms of change in nonviolent struggle (discussed below). Nonviolent discipline is also extremely important in the process of political jiu-jitsu. In this process the stark brutality of the regime against the clearly nonviolent actionists politically rebounds against the dictators' position, causing dissention in their own ranks as well as fomenting support for the resisters among the general population, the regime's usual supporters, and third parties.

In some cases, however, limited violence against the dictatorship may be inevitable. Frustration and hatred of the regime may explode into violence. Or, certain groups may be unwilling to abandon violent means even though they recognize the important role of nonviolent struggle. In these cases, political defiance does not need to be abandoned. However, it will be necessary to separate the violent action as far as possible from the nonviolent action. This should be done in terms of geography, population groups, timing, and issues. Otherwise the violence could have a disastrous effect on the potentially much more powerful and successful use of political defiance.

The historical record indicates that while casualties in dead and wounded must be expected in political defiance, they will be far fewer than the casualties in military warfare. Furthermore, this type of struggle does not contribute to the endless cycle of killing and brutality.

Nonviolent struggle both requires and tends to produce a loss (or greater control) of fear of the government and its violent repression. That abandonment or control of fear is a key element in destroying the power of the dictators over the general population.

Openness, secrecy, and high standards

Secrecy, deception, and underground conspiracy pose very difficult problems for a movement using nonviolent action. It is often impossible to keep the political police and intelligence agents from learning about intentions and plans. From the perspective of the movement, secrecy is not only rooted in fear but contributes to fear, which dampens the spirit of resistance and reduces the number of people who can participate in a given action. It also can contribute to suspicions and accusations, often unjustified, within the movement, concerning who is an informer or agent for the opponents. Secrecy may also affect the ability of a movement to remain nonviolent. In contrast, openness regarding intentions and plans will not only have the opposite effects, but will contribute to an image that the resistance movement is in fact extremely powerful. The problem is of course more complex than this suggests, and there are significant aspects of resistance activities that may require secrecy. A well-informed assessment will be required by those knowledgeable about both the dynamics of nonviolent struggle and also the dictatorship's means of surveillance in the specific situation.

The editing, printing, and distribution of underground publications, the use of illegal radio broadcasts from within the country, and the gathering of intelligence about the operations of the dictatorship are among the special limited types of activities where a high degree of secrecy will be required.

The maintenance of high standards of behavior in nonviolent action is necessary at all stages of the conflict. Such factors as fearlessness and maintaining nonviolent discipline are always required. It is important to remember that large numbers of people may frequently be necessary to effect particular changes. However, such numbers can be obtained as reliable participants only by maintaining the high standards of the movement.

Shifting power relationships

Strategists need to remember that the conflict in which political defiance is applied is a constantly changing field of struggle with continuing interplay of moves and countermoves. Nothing is static. Power relationships, both absolute and relative, are subject to constant and rapid changes. This is made possible by the resisters continuing their nonviolent persistence despite repression.

The variations in the respective power of the contending sides in this type of conflict situation are likely to be more extreme than in violent conflicts, to take place more quickly, and to have more diverse and politically significant consequences. Due to these variations, specific actions by the resisters are likely to have consequences far beyond the particular time and place in which they occur. These effects will rebound to strengthen or weaken one group or another.

In addition, the nonviolent group may, by its actions exert influence over the increase or decrease in the relative strength of *the opponent group* to a great extent. For example, disciplined courageous nonviolent resistance in face of the dictators' brutalities may induce unease, disaffection, unreliability, and in extreme situations even mutiny among the dictators' own soldiers and population. This resistance may also result in increased international condemnation of the dictatorship. In addition, skillful, disciplined, and persistent use of political defiance may result in more and more participation in the resistance by people who normally would give their tacit support to the dictators or generally remain neutral in the conflict.

Four mechanisms of change

Nonviolent struggle produces change in four ways. The first mechanism is the least likely, though it has occurred. When members of the opponent group are emotionally moved by the suffering of repression imposed on courageous nonviolent resisters or are rationally persuaded that the resisters' cause is just, they may come to accept the resisters' aims. This mechanism is called conversion. Though cases of *conversion* in nonviolent action do sometimes happen, they are rare, and in most conflicts this does not occur at all or at least not on a significant scale.

Far more often, nonviolent struggle operates by changing the conflict situation and the society so that the opponents simply cannot do as they like. It is this change that produces the other three mechanisms: accommodation, nonviolent coercion, and disintegration. Which of these occurs depends on the degree to which the relative and absolute power relations are shifted in favor of the democrats.

If the issues are not fundamental ones, the demands of the opposition in a limited campaign are not considered threatening, and the contest of forces has altered the power relationships to some degree, the immediate conflict may be ended by reaching an agreement, a splitting of differences or compromise. This mechanism is called *accommodation*. Many strikes are settled in this manner, for example, with both sides attaining some of their objectives but neither achieving all it wanted. A government may perceive such a settlement to have some positive benefits, such as defusing tension, creating an impression of "fairness," or polishing the international image of the regime. It is important, therefore, that great care be exercised in selecting the issues on which a settlement by accommodation is acceptable. A struggle to bring down a dictatorship is not one of these.

Nonviolent struggle can be much more powerful than indicated by the mechanisms of conversion or accommodation. Mass noncooperation and defiance can so change social and political situations, especially power relationships, that the dictators' ability to control the economic, social, and political processes of government and the society is in fact taken away. The opponents' military forces may become so unreliable that they no longer simply obey orders to repress resisters. Although the opponents' leaders remain in their positions, and adhere to their original goals, their ability to act effectively has been taken away from them. That is called *nonviolent coercion*.

In some extreme situations, the conditions producing nonviolent coercion are carried still further. The opponents' leadership in fact loses all ability to act and their own structure of power collapses. The resisters' self-direction, noncooperation, and defiance become so complete that the opponents now lack even a semblance of control over them. The opponents' bureaucracy refuses to obey its own leadership. The opponents' troops and police mutiny. The opponents' usual supporters or population repudiate their former leadership, denying that they have any right to rule at all. Hence, their former assistance and obedience falls away. The fourth mechanism of change, *disintegration* of the opponents' system, is so complete that they do not even have sufficient power to surrender. The regime simply falls to pieces.

In planning liberation strategies, these four mechanisms should be kept in mind. They sometimes operate essentially by chance. However, the selection of one or more of these as the intended mechanism of change in a conflict will make it possible to formulate specific and mutually reinforcing strategies. Which mechanism (or mechanisms) to select will depend on numerous factors, including the absolute and relative power of the contending groups and the attitudes and objectives of the nonviolent struggle group.

Democratizing effects of political defiance

In contrast to the centralizing effects of violent sanctions, use of the technique of nonviolent struggle contributes to democratizing the political society in several ways.

One part of the democratizing effect is negative. That is, in contrast to military means, this technique does not provide a means of repression under command of a ruling elite which can be turned against the population to establish or maintain a dictatorship. Leaders of a political defiance movement can exert influence and apply pressures on their followers, but they cannot imprison or execute them when they dissent or choose other leaders.

Another part of the democratizing effect is positive. That is, nonviolent struggle provides the population with means of resistance that can be used to achieve and defend their liberties against existing or would-be dictators. Below are several of the positive democratizing effects nonviolent struggle may have:

- Experience in applying nonviolent struggle may result in the population being more self-confident in challenging the regime's threats and capacity for violent repression.

- Nonviolent struggle provides the means of noncooperation and defiance by which the population can resist undemocratic controls over them by any dictatorial group.

- Nonviolent struggle can be used to assert the practice of democratic freedoms, such as free speech, free press, independent organizations, and free assembly, in face of repressive controls.

- Nonviolent struggle contributes strongly to the survival, re-birth, and strengthening of the independent groups and in-stitutions of the society, as previously discussed. These are important for democracy because of their capacity to mobi-lize the power capacity of the population and to impose lim-its on the effective power of any would-be dictators.

- Nonviolent struggle provides means by which the popula-tion can wield power against repressive police and military action by a dictatorial government.

- Nonviolent struggle provides methods by which the popu-lation and the independent institutions can in the interests of democracy restrict or sever the sources of power for the ruling elite, thereby threatening its capacity to continue its domination.

Complexity of nonviolent struggle

As we have seen from this discussion, nonviolent struggle is a com-plex technique of social action, involving a multitude of methods, a range of mechanisms of change, and specific behavioral require-ments. To be effective, especially against a dictatorship, political defiance requires careful planning and preparation. Prospective participants will need to understand what is required of them. Resources will need to have been made available. And strategists will need to have analyzed how nonviolent struggle can be most effectively applied. We now turn our attention to this latter crucial element: the need for strategic planning.

SIX
THE NEED FOR STRATEGIC PLANNING

Political defiance campaigns against dictatorships may begin in a variety of ways. In the past these struggles have almost always been unplanned and essentially accidental. Specific grievances that have triggered past initial actions have varied widely, but often included new brutalities, the arrest or killing of a highly regarded person, a new repressive policy or order, food shortages, disrespect toward religious beliefs, or an anniversary of an important related event. Sometimes, a particular act by the dictatorship has so enraged the populace that they have launched into action without having any idea how the rising might end. At other times a courageous individual or a small group may have taken action which aroused support. A specific grievance may be recognized by others as similar to wrongs they had experienced and they, too, may thus join the struggle. Sometimes, a specific call for resistance from a small group or individual may meet an unexpectedly large response.

While spontaneity has some positive qualities, it has often had disadvantages. Frequently, the democratic resisters have not anticipated the brutalities of the dictatorship, so that they suffered gravely and the resistance has collapsed. At times the lack of planning by democrats has left crucial decisions to chance, with disastrous results. Even when the oppressive system was brought down, lack of planning on how to handle the transition to a democratic system has contributed to the emergence of a new dictatorship.

Realistic planning

In the future, unplanned popular action will undoubtedly play significant roles in risings against dictatorships. However, it is now possible to calculate the most effective ways to bring down a dictatorship, to assess when the political situation and popular mood are ripe, and to choose how to initiate a campaign. Very careful thought *based on a realistic assessment* of the situation and the capabilities of the populace is required in order to select effective ways to achieve freedom under such circumstances.

If one wishes to accomplish something, it is wise to plan how to do it. The more important the goal, or the graver the consequences of failure, the more important planning becomes. Strategic planning increases the likelihood that all available resources will be mobilized and employed most effectively. This is especially true for a democratic movement – which has limited material resources and whose supporters will be in danger – that is trying to bring down a powerful dictatorship. In contrast, the dictatorship usually will have access to vast material resources, organizational strength, and ability to perpetrate brutalities.

"To plan a strategy" here means to calculate a course of action that will make it more likely to get from the present to the desired future situation. In terms of this discussion, it means from a dictatorship to a future democratic system. A plan to achieve that objective will usually consist of a phased series of campaigns and other organized activities designed to strengthen the oppressed population and society and to weaken the dictatorship. Note here that the objective is not simply to destroy the current dictatorship but to emplace a democratic system. A grand strategy that limits its objective to merely destroying the incumbent dictatorship runs a great risk of producing another tyrant.

Hurdles to planning

Some exponents of freedom in various parts of the world do not bring their full capacities to bear on the problem of how to achieve liberation. Only rarely do these advocates fully recognize the extreme importance of careful strategic planning before they act. Consequently, this is almost never done.

Why is it that the people who have the vision of bringing political freedom to their people should so rarely prepare a comprehensive strategic plan to achieve that goal? Unfortunately, often most people in democratic opposition groups do not understand the need for strategic planning or are not accustomed or trained to think strategically. This is a difficult task. Constantly harassed by the dictatorship, and overwhelmed by immediate responsibilities, resistance leaders often do not have the safety or time to develop strategic thinking skills.

Instead, it is a common pattern simply to react to the initiatives of the dictatorship. The opposition is then always on the defensive, seeking to maintain limited liberties or bastions of freedom, at best slowing the advance of the dictatorial controls or causing certain problems for the regime's new policies.

Some individuals and groups, of course, may not see the need for broad long-term planning of a liberation movement. Instead, they may naïvely think that if they simply espouse their goal strongly, firmly, and long enough, it will somehow come to pass. Others assume that if they simply live and witness according to their principles and ideals in face of difficulties, they are doing all they can to implement them. The espousal of humane goals and loyalty to ideals are admirable, but are grossly inadequate to end a dictatorship and to achieve freedom.

Other opponents of dictatorship may naïvely think that if only they use enough violence, freedom will come. But, as noted earlier, violence is no guarantor of success. Instead of liberation, it can lead to defeat, massive tragedy, or both. In most situations the dictatorship is best equipped for violent struggle and the military realities rarely, if ever, favor the democrats.

There are also activists who base their actions on what they "feel" they should do. These approaches are, however, not only egocentric but they offer no guidance for developing a grand strategy of liberation.

Action based on a "bright idea" that someone has had is also limited. What is needed instead is action based on careful calculation of the "next steps" required to topple the dictatorship. Without strategic analysis, resistance leaders will often not know what that "next step" should be, for they have not thought carefully about the successive specific steps required to achieve victory. Creativity and bright ideas are very important, but they need to be utilized in order to advance the strategic situation of the democratic forces.

Acutely aware of the multitude of actions that could be taken against the dictatorship and unable to determine where to begin, some people counsel "Do everything simultaneously." That might be helpful but, of course, is impossible, especially for relatively weak movements. Furthermore, such an approach provides no guidance on where to begin, on where to concentrate efforts, and how to use often limited resources.

Other persons and groups may see the need for some planning, but are only able to think about it on a short-term or tactical basis. They may not see that longer-term planning is necessary or possible. They may at times be unable to think and analyze in strategic terms, allowing themselves to be repeatedly distracted by relatively small issues, often responding to the opponents' actions rather than seizing the initiative for the democratic resistance. Devoting so much energy to short-term activities, these leaders often fail to explore several alternative courses of action which could guide the overall efforts so that the goal is constantly approached.

It is also just possible that some democratic movements do not plan a comprehensive strategy to bring down the dictatorship, concentrating instead only on immediate issues, for another reason. Inside themselves, they do not really believe that the dictatorship can be ended by their own efforts. Therefore, planning how to do so is considered to be a romantic waste of time or an exercise in futility. People struggling for freedom against established brutal dictatorships are often confronted by such immense military and police power that it appears the dictators can accomplish whatever they will. Lacking real hope, these people will, nevertheless, defy the dictatorship for reasons of integrity and perhaps history. Though they will never admit it, perhaps never consciously recognize it, their actions appear to themselves as hopeless. Hence, for them, long-term comprehensive strategic planning has no merit.

The result of such failures to plan strategically is often drastic: one's strength is dissipated, one's actions are ineffective, energy is wasted on minor issues, advantages are not utilized, and sacrifices are for naught. If democrats do not plan strategically they are likely to fail to achieve their objectives. A poorly planned, odd mixture of activities will not move a major resistance effort forward. Instead, it will more likely allow the dictatorship to increase its controls and power.

Unfortunately, because comprehensive strategic plans for liberation are rarely, if ever, developed, dictatorships appear much more durable than they in fact are. They survive for years or decades longer than need be the case.

Four important terms in strategic planning

In order to help us to think strategically, clarity about the meanings of four basic terms is important.

Grand strategy is the conception that serves to coordinate and direct the use of all appropriate and available resources (economic, human, moral, political, organizational, etc.) of a group seeking to attain its objectives in a conflict.

Grand strategy, by focusing primary attention on the group's objectives and resources in the conflict, determines the most appropriate technique of action (such as conventional military warfare or nonviolent struggle) to be employed in the conflict. In planning a grand strategy resistance leaders must evaluate and plan which pressures and influences are to be brought to bear upon the opponents. Further, grand strategy will include decisions on the appropriate conditions and timing under which initial and subsequent resistance campaigns will be launched.

Grand strategy sets the basic framework for the selection of more limited strategies for waging the struggle. Grand strategy also determines the allocation of general tasks to particular groups and the distribution of resources to them for use in the struggle.

Strategy is the conception of how best to achieve particular objectives in a conflict, operating within the scope of the chosen grand strategy. Strategy is concerned with whether, when, and how to fight, as well as how to achieve maximum effectiveness in struggling for certain ends. A strategy has been compared to the artist's concept, while a strategic plan is the architect's blueprint.[12]

---

[12] Robert Helvey, personal communication, 15 August 1993.

Strategy may also include efforts to develop a strategic situation that is so advantageous that the opponents are able to foresee that open conflict is likely to bring their certain defeat, and therefore capitulate without an open struggle. Or, if not, the improved strategic situation will make success of the challengers certain in struggle. Strategy also involves how to act to make good use of successes when gained.

Applied to the course of the struggle itself, the strategic plan is the basic idea of how a campaign shall develop, and how its separate components shall be fitted together to contribute most advantageously to achieve its objectives. It involves the skillful deployment of particular action groups in smaller operations. Planning for a wise strategy must take into consideration the requirements for success in the operation of the chosen technique of struggle. Different techniques will have different requirements. Of course, just fulfilling "requirements" is not sufficient to ensure success. Additional factors may also be needed.

In devising strategies, the democrats must clearly define their objectives and determine how to measure the effectiveness of efforts to achieve them. This definition and analysis permits the strategist to identify the precise requirements for securing each selected objective. This need for clarity and definition applies equally to tactical planning.

Tactics and methods of action are used to implement the strategy. *Tactics* relate to the skillful use of one's forces to the best advantage in a limited situation. A tactic is a limited action, employed to achieve a restricted objective. The choice of tactics is governed by the conception of how best in a restricted phase of a conflict to utilize the available means of fighting to implement the strategy. To be most effective, tactics and methods must be chosen and applied with constant attention to the achievement of strategic objectives. Tactical gains that do not reinforce the attainment of strategic objectives may in the end turn out to be wasted energy.

A tactic is thus concerned with a limited course of action that fits within the broad strategy, just as a strategy fits within the grand strategy. Tactics are always concerned with fighting, whereas strategy includes wider considerations. A particular tactic can only be understood as part of the overall strategy of a battle or a campaign. Tactics are applied for shorter periods of time than strategies, or in smaller areas (geographical, institutional, etc.), or by a more limited number of people, or for more limited objectives. In nonviolent action the distinction between a tactical objective and a strategic objective may be partly indicated by whether the chosen objective of the action is minor or major.

Offensive tactical engagements are selected to support attainment of strategic objectives. Tactical engagements are the tools of the strategist in creating conditions favorable for delivering decisive attacks against an opponent. It is most important, therefore, that those given responsibility for planning and executing tactical operations be skilled in assessing the situation, and selecting the most appropriate methods for it. Those expected to participate must be trained in the use of the chosen technique and the specific methods.

Method refers to the specific weapons or means of action. Within the technique of nonviolent struggle, these include the dozens of particular forms of action (such as the many kinds of strikes, boycotts, political noncooperation, and the like) cited in Chapter Five. (See also Appendix.)

The development of a responsible and effective strategic plan for a nonviolent struggle depends upon the careful formulation and selection of the grand strategy, strategies, tactics, and methods.

The main lesson of this discussion is that a calculated use of one's intellect is required in careful strategic planning for liberation from a dictatorship. Failure to plan intelligently can contribute to disasters, while the effective use of one's intellectual capacities can chart a strategic course that will judiciously utilize one's available resources to move the society toward the goal of liberty and democracy.

SEVEN
PLANNING STRATEGY

In order to increase the chances for success, resistance leaders will need to formulate a comprehensive plan of action capable of strengthening the suffering people, weakening and then destroying the dictatorship, and building a durable democracy. To achieve such a plan of action, a careful assessment of the situation and of the options for effective action is needed. Out of such a careful analysis both a grand strategy and the specific campaign strategies for achieving freedom can be developed. Though related, the development of grand strategy and campaign strategies are two separate processes. Only after the grand strategy has been developed can the specific campaign strategies be fully developed. Campaign strategies will need to be designed to achieve and reinforce the grand strategic objectives.

The development of resistance strategy requires attention to many questions and tasks. Here we shall identify some of the important factors that need to be considered, both at the grand strategic level and the level of campaign strategy. All strategic planning, however, requires that the resistance planners have a profound understanding of the entire conflict situation, including attention to physical, historical, governmental, military, cultural, social, political, psychological, economic, and international factors. Strategies can only be developed in the context of the particular struggle and its background.

Of primary importance, democratic leaders and strategic planners will want to assess the objectives and importance of the cause. Are the objectives worth a major struggle, and why? It is critical to determine the real objective of the struggle. We have argued here that overthrow of the dictatorship or removal of the present dictators is *not* enough. The objective in these conflicts needs to be the establishment of a free society with a democratic system of government. Clarity on this point will influence the development of a grand strategy and of the ensuing specific strategies.

Particularly, strategists will need to answer many fundamental questions, such as these:

- What are the main obstacles to achieving freedom?

- What factors will facilitate achieving freedom?

- What are the main strengths of the dictatorship?

- What are the various weaknesses of the dictatorship?

- To what degree are the sources of power for the dictatorship vulnerable?

- What are the strengths of the democratic forces and the general population?

- What are the weaknesses of the democratic forces and how can they be corrected?

- What is the status of third parties, not immediately involved in the conflict, who already assist or might assist, either the dictatorship or the democratic movement, and if so in what ways?

Choice of means

At the grand strategic level, planners will need to choose the main means of struggle to be employed in the coming conflict. The merits and limitations of several alternative techniques of struggle will need to be evaluated, such as conventional military warfare, guerrilla warfare, political defiance, and others.

In making this choice the strategists will need to consider such questions as the following: Is the chosen type of struggle within the capacities of the democrats? Does the chosen technique utilize strengths of the dominated population? Does this technique target the weaknesses of the dictatorship, or does it strike at its strongest points? Do the means help the democrats become more self-reliant, or do they require dependency on third parties or external suppliers? What is the record of the use of the chosen means in bringing down dictatorships? Do they increase or limit the casualties and destruction that may be incurred in the coming conflict? Assuming success in ending the dictatorship, what effect would the selected means have on the type of government that would arise from the struggle? The types of action determined to be counterproductive will need to be excluded in the developed grand strategy.

In previous chapters we have argued that political defiance offers significant comparative advantages to other techniques of struggle. Strategists will need to examine their particular conflict situation and determine whether political defiance provides affirmative answers to the above questions.

Planning for democracy

It should be remembered that against a dictatorship the objective of the grand strategy is not simply to bring down the dictators but to install a democratic system and make the rise of a new dictatorship impossible. To accomplish these objectives, the chosen means of struggle will need to contribute to a change in the distribution of effective power in the society. Under the dictatorship the population and civil institutions of the society have been too weak, and the government too strong. Without a change in this imbalance, a new set of rulers can, if they wish, be just as dictatorial as the old ones. A "palace revolution" or a coup d'état therefore is not welcome.

Political defiance contributes to a more equitable distribution of effective power through the mobilization of the society against the dictatorship, as was discussed in Chapter Five. This process occurs in several ways. The development of a nonviolent struggle capacity means that the dictatorship's capacity for violent repression no longer as easily produces intimidation and submission among the population. The population will have at its disposal powerful means to counter and at times block the exertion of the dictators' power. Further, the mobilization of popular power through political defiance will strengthen the independent institutions of the society. The experience of once exercising effective power is not quickly forgot. The knowledge and skill gained in struggle will make the population less likely to be easily dominated by would-be dictators. This shift in power relationships would ultimately make establishment of a durable democratic society much more likely.

External assistance

As part of the preparation of a grand strategy it is necessary to assess what will be the relative roles of internal resistance and external pressures for disintegrating the dictatorship. In this analysis we have argued that the main force of the struggle must be borne from inside the country itself. To the degree that international assistance comes at all, it will be stimulated by the internal struggle.

As a modest supplement, efforts can be made to mobilize world public opinion against the dictatorship, on humanitarian, moral, and religious grounds. Efforts can be taken to obtain diplomatic, political, and economic sanctions by governments and international organizations against the dictatorship. These may take the forms of economic and military weapons embargoes, reduction in levels of diplomatic recognition or the breaking of diplomatic ties, banning of economic assistance and prohibition of investments in the dictatorial country, expulsion of the dictatorial government from various international organizations and from United Nations bodies. Further, international assistance, such as the provision of financial and communications support, can also be provided directly to the democratic forces.

Formulating a grand strategy

Following an assessment of the situation, the choice of means, and a determination of the role of external assistance, planners of the grand strategy will need to sketch in broad strokes how the conflict might best be conducted. This broad plan would stretch from the present to the future liberation and the institution of a democratic system.

In formulating a grand strategy these planners will need to ask themselves a variety of questions. The following questions pose (in a more specific way than earlier) the types of considerations required in devising a grand strategy for a political defiance struggle:

How might the long-term struggle best begin? How can the oppressed population muster sufficient self-confidence and strength to act to challenge the dictatorship, even initially in a limited way? How could the population's capacity to apply noncooperation and defiance be increased with time and experience? What might be the objectives of a series of limited campaigns to regain democratic control over the society and limit the dictatorship?

Are there independent institutions that have survived the dictatorship which might be used in the struggle to establish freedom? What institutions of the society can be regained from the dictators' control, or what institutions need to be newly created by the democrats to meet their needs and establish spheres of democracy even while the dictatorship continues?

How can organizational strength in the resistance be developed? How can participants be trained? What resources (finances, equipment, etc.) will be required throughout the struggle? What types of symbolism can be most effective in mobilizing the population?

By what kinds of action and in what stages could the sources of power of the dictators be incrementally weakened and severed? How can the resisting population simultaneously persist in its defiance and also maintain the necessary nonviolent discipline? How can the society continue to meet its basic needs during the course of the struggle? How can social order be maintained in the midst of the conflict? As victory approaches, how can the democratic resistance continue to build the institutional base of the post-dictatorship society to make the transition as smooth as possible?

It must be remembered that no single blueprint exists or can be created to plan strategy for every liberation movement against dictatorships. Each struggle to bring down a dictatorship and establish a democratic system will be somewhat different. No two situations will be exactly alike, each dictatorship will have some individual characteristics, and the capacities of the freedom-seeking population

will vary. Planners of grand strategy for a political defiance struggle
will require a profound understanding not only of their specific
conflict situation, but of their chosen means of struggle as well.[13]
    When the grand strategy of the struggle has been carefully
planned there are sound reasons for making it widely known. The
large numbers of people required to participate may be more willing
and able to act if they understand the general conception, as well
as specific instructions. This knowledge could potentially have a
very positive effect on their morale, their willingness to participate,
and to act appropriately. The general outlines of the grand strategy
would become known to the dictators in any case and knowledge
of its features potentially could lead them to be less brutal in their
repression, knowing that it could rebound politically against themselves. Awareness of the special characteristics of the grand strategy
could potentially also contribute to dissension and defections from
the dictators' own camp.
    Once a grand strategic plan for bringing down the dictator-
ship and establishing a democratic system has been adopted, it is
important for the pro-democracy groups to persist in applying it.
Only in very rare circumstances should the struggle depart from
the initial grand strategy. When there is abundant evidence that the
chosen grand strategy was misconceived, or that the circumstances
of the struggle have fundamentally changed, planners may need to
alter the grand strategy. Even then, this should be done only after a
basic reassessment has been made and a new more adequate grand
strategic plan has been developed and adopted.

---

[13] Recommended full length studies are Gene Sharp, *The Politics of Nonviolent Action*
of Nonviolent Action, (Boston, Massachusetts: Porter Sargent, 1973) and Peter Acker-
man and Christopher Kruegler, *Strategic Nonviolent Conflict*, (Westport, Connecticut:
Praeger, 1994). Also see Gene Sharp, *Waging Nonviolent Stuggle: Twentieth Century*
Practice and Twenty-First Century Potential. Boston: Porter Sargent, 2005.

Planning campaign strategies

However wise and promising the developed grand strategy to end the dictatorship and to institute democracy may be, a grand strategy does not implement itself. Particular strategies will need to be developed to guide the major campaigns aimed at undermining the dictators' power. These strategies, in turn, will incorporate and guide a range of tactical engagements that will aim to strike decisive blows against the dictators' regime. The tactics and the specific methods of action must be chosen carefully so that they contribute to achieving the goals of each particular strategy. The discussion here focuses exclusively on the level of strategy.

Strategists planning the major campaigns will, like those who planned the grand strategy, require a thorough understanding of the nature and modes of operation of their chosen technique of struggle. Just as military officers must understand force structures, tactics, logistics, munitions, the effects of geography, and the like in order to plot military strategy, political defiance planners must understand the nature and strategic principles of nonviolent struggle. Even then, however, knowledge of nonviolent struggle, attention to recommendations in this essay, and answers to the questions posed here will not themselves produce strategies. The formulation of strategies for the struggle still requires an informed creativity.

In planning the strategies for the specific selective resistance campaigns and for the longer term development of the liberation struggle, the political defiance strategists will need to consider various issues and problems. The following are among these:

- Determination of the specific objectives of the campaign and their contributions to implementing the grand strategy.

- Consideration of the specific methods, or political weapons, that can best be used to implement the chosen strategies. Within each overall plan for a particular strategic campaign it will be necessary to determine what smaller, tactical plans and which specific methods of action should be used to impose pressures and restrictions against the dictatorship's sources of power. It should be remembered that the achievement of major objectives will come as a result of carefully chosen and implemented specific smaller steps.

- Determination whether, or how, economic issues should be related to the overall essentially political struggle. If economic issues are to be prominent in the struggle, care will be needed that the economic grievances can actually be remedied after the dictatorship is ended. Otherwise, disillusionment and disaffection may set in if quick solutions are not provided during the transition period to a democratic society. Such disillusionment could facilitate the rise of dictatorial forces promising an end to economic woes.

- Determination in advance of what kind of leadership structure and communications system will work best for initiating the resistance struggle. What means of decision-making and communication will be possible during the course of the struggle to give continuing guidance to the resisters and the general population?

- Communication of the resistance news to the general population, to the dictators' forces, and the international press. Claims and reporting should always be strictly factual. Exaggerations and unfounded claims will undermine the credibility of the resistance.

- Plans for self-reliant constructive social, educational, economic, and political activities to meet the needs of one's own people during the coming conflict. Such projects can be conducted by persons not directly involved in the resistance activities.

- Determination of what kind of external assistance is desirable in support of the specific campaign or the general liberation struggle. How can external help be best mobilized and used without making the internal struggle dependent on uncertain external factors? Attention will need to be given to which external groups are most likely, and most appropriate, to assist, such as non-governmental organizations (social movements, religious or political groups, labor unions, etc.), governments, and/or the United Nations and its various bodies.

Furthermore, the resistance planners will need to take measures to preserve order and to meet social needs by one's own forces during mass resistance against dictatorial controls. This will not only create alternative independent democratic structures and meet genuine needs, but also will reduce credibility for any claims that ruthless repression is required to halt disorder and lawlessness.

Spreading the idea of noncooperation

For successful political defiance against a dictatorship, it is essential that the population grasp the idea of noncooperation. As illustrated by the "Monkey Master" story (see Chapter Three), the basic idea is simple: if enough of the subordinates refuse to continue their cooperation long enough despite repression, the oppressive system will be weakened and finally collapse.

People living under the dictatorship may be already familiar with this concept from a variety of sources. Even so, the democratic forces should deliberately spread and popularize the idea of noncooperation. The "Monkey Master" story, or a similar one, could be disseminated throughout the society. Such a story could be easily understood. Once the general concept of noncooperation is grasped, people will be able to understand the relevance of future calls to practice noncooperation with the dictatorship. They will also be able on their own to improvise a myriad of specific forms of noncooperation in new situations.

Despite the difficulties and dangers in attempts to communicate ideas, news, and resistance instructions while living under dictatorships, democrats have frequently proved this to be possible.

Even under Nazi and Communist rule it was possible for resisters to communicate not only with other individuals but even with large public audiences through the production of illegal newspapers, leaflets, books, and in later years with audio and video cassettes.

With the advantage of prior strategic planning, general guidelines for resistance can be prepared and disseminated. These can indicate the issues and circumstances under which the population should protest and withhold cooperation, and how this might be done. Then, even if communications from the democratic leadership are severed, and specific instructions have not been issued or received, the population will know how to act on certain important issues. Such guidelines would also provide a test to identify counterfeit "resistance instructions" issued by the political police designed to provoke discrediting action.

Repression and countermeasures

Strategic planners will need to assess the likely responses and repression, especially the threshold of violence, of the dictatorship to the actions of the democratic resistance. It will be necessary to determine how to withstand, counteract, or avoid this possible increased repression without submission. Tactically, for specific occasions, appropriate warnings to the population and the resisters about expected repression would be in order, so that they will know the risks of participation. If repression may be serious, preparations for medical assistance for wounded resisters should be made.

Anticipating repression, the strategists will do well to consider in advance the use of tactics and methods that will contribute to achieving the specific goal of a campaign, or liberation, but that will make brutal repression less likely or less possible. For example, street demonstrations and parades against extreme dictatorships may be dramatic, but they may also risk thousands of dead demonstrators. The high cost to the demonstrators may not, however, actually apply more pressure on the dictatorship than would occur through everyone staying home, a strike, or massive acts of noncooperation from the civil servants.

If it has been proposed that provocative resistance action risking high casualties will be required for a strategic purpose, then one should very carefully consider the proposal's costs and possible gains. Will the population and the resisters be likely to behave in a disciplined and nonviolent manner during the course of the struggle? Can they resist provocations to violence? Planners must consider what measures may be taken to keep nonviolent discipline and maintain the resistance despite brutalities. Will such measures as pledges, policy statements, discipline leaflets, marshals for demonstrations, and boycotts of pro-violence persons and groups be possible and effective? Leaders should always be alert for the presence of *agents provocateurs* whose mission will be to incite the demonstrators to violence.

Adhering to the strategic plan

Once a sound strategic plan is in place, the democratic forces should not be distracted by minor moves of the dictators that may tempt them to depart from the grand strategy and the strategy for a particular campaign, causing them to focus major activities on unimportant issues. Nor should the emotions of the moment — perhaps in response to new brutalities by the dictatorship — be allowed to divert the democratic resistance from its grand strategy or the campaign strategy. The brutalities may have been perpetrated precisely in order to provoke the democratic forces to abandon their well-laid plan and even to commit violent acts in order that the dictators could more easily defeat them.

As long as the basic analysis is judged to be sound, the task of the pro-democracy forces is to press forward stage by stage. Of course, changes in tactics and intermediate objectives will occur and good leaders will always be ready to exploit opportunities. These adjustments should not be confused with objectives of the grand strategy or the objectives of the specific campaign. Careful implementation of the chosen grand strategy and of strategies for particular campaigns will greatly contribute to success.

EIGHT
APPLYING POLITICAL DEFIANCE

In situations in which the population feels powerless and frightened, it is important that initial tasks for the public be low-risk, confidence-building actions. These types of actions — such as wearing one's clothes in an unusual way — may publicly register a dissenting opinion and provide an opportunity for the public to participate significantly in acts of dissent. In other cases a relatively minor (on the surface) nonpolitical issue (such as securing a safe water supply) might be made the focus for group action. Strategists should choose an issue the merits of which will be widely recognized and difficult to reject. Success in such limited campaigns could not only correct specific grievances but also convince the population that it indeed has power potential.

Most of the strategies of campaigns in the long-term struggle should *not* aim for the immediate complete downfall of the dictatorship, but instead for gaining limited objectives. Nor does every campaign require the participation of all sections of the population.

In contemplating a series of specific campaigns to implement the grand strategy, the defiance strategists need to consider how the campaigns at the beginning, the middle, and near the conclusion of the long-term struggle will differ from each other.

Selective resistance

In the initial stages of the struggle, separate campaigns with diffe ent specific objectives can be very useful. Such selective campai may follow one after the other. Occasionally, two or three overlap in time.

In planning a strategy for "selective resistance" it is to identify specific limited issues or grievances that syr general oppression of the dictatorship. Such issues m propriate targets for conducting campaigns to gair strategic objectives within the overall grand strate'

These intermediary strategic objectives need to be attainable by the current or projected power capacity of the democratic forces. This helps to ensure a series of victories, which are good for morale, and also contribute to advantageous incremental shifts in power relations for the long-term struggle.

Selective resistance strategies should concentrate primarily on specific social, economic, or political issues. These may be chosen in order to keep some part of the social and political system out of the dictators' control, to regain control of some part currently controlled by the dictators, or to deny the dictators a particular objective. If possible, the campaign of selective resistance should also strike at one weakness or more of the dictatorship, as already discussed. Thereby, democrats can make the greatest possible impact with their available power capacity.

Very early the strategists need to plan at least the strategy for the first campaign. What are to be its limited objectives? How will it help fulfill the chosen grand strategy? If possible, it is wise to formulate at least the general outlines of strategies for a second and possibly a third campaign. All such strategies will need to implement the chosen grand strategy and operate within its general guidelines.

Symbolic challenge

At the beginning of a new campaign to undermine the dictatorship, the first more specifically political actions may be limited in scope. They should be designed in part to test and influence the mood of the population, and to prepare them for continuing struggle through cooperation and political defiance.

The initial action is likely to take the form of symbolic protest be a symbolic act of limited or temporary noncooperation. number of persons willing to act is small, then the initial act example, involve placing flowers at a place of symbolic On the other hand, if the number of persons willing to then a five minute halt to all activities or several might be used. In other situations, a few individuals might undertake a hunger strike, a vigil at a place of symbolic importance, a brief student boycott of classes, or a temporary sit-in at an important office. Under a dictatorship these more aggressive actions would most likely be met with harsh repression.

Certain symbolic acts, such as a physical occupation in front of the dictator's palace or political police headquarters may involve high risk and are therefore not advisable for initiating a campaign.

Initial symbolic protest actions have at times aroused major national and international attention — as the mass street demonstrations in Burma in 1988 or the student occupation and hunger strike in Tiananman Square in Beijing in 1989. The high casualties of demonstrators in both of these cases points to the great care strategists must exercise in planning campaigns. Although having a tremendous moral and psychological impact, such actions by themselves are unlikely to bring down a dictatorship, for they remain largely symbolic and do not alter the power position of the dictatorship.

It usually is not possible to sever the availability of the sources of power to the dictators completely and rapidly at the beginning of a struggle. That would require virtually the whole population and almost all the institutions of the society — which had previously been largely submissive — to reject absolutely the regime and suddenly defy it by massive and strong noncooperation. That has not yet occurred and would be most difficult to achieve. In most cases, therefore, a quick campaign of full noncooperation and defiance is an unrealistic strategy for an early campaign against the dictatorship.

Spreading responsibility

During a selective resistance campaign the brunt of the struggle is for a time usually borne by one section or more of the population. In a later campaign with a different objective, the burden of the struggle would be shifted to other population groups. For example, students might conduct strikes on an educational issue, religiou leaders and believers might concentrate on a freedom of religic issue, rail workers might meticulously obey safety regulations sc to slow down the rail transport system, journalists might challe

censorship by publishing papers with blank spaces in which prohib-
ited articles would have appeared, or police might repeatedly fail
to locate and arrest wanted members of the democratic opposition.
Phasing resistance campaigns by issue and population group will
allow certain segments of the population to rest while resistance
continues.

Selective resistance is especially important *to defend* the existence and autonomy of independent social, economic, and political
groups and institutions outside the control of the dictatorship, which
were briefly discussed earlier. These centers of power provide the
institutional bases from which the population can exert pressure or
can resist dictatorial controls. In the struggle, they are likely to be
among the first targets of the dictatorship.

Aiming at the dictators' power

As the long-term struggle develops beyond the initial strategies into
more ambitious and advanced phases, the strategists will need to
calculate how the dictators' sources of power can be further restricted.
The aim would be to use popular noncooperation to create a new
more advantageous strategic situation for the democratic forces.

As the democratic resistance forces gained strength, strategists
would plot more ambitious noncooperation and defiance to sever
the dictatorships' sources of power, with the goal of producing increasing political paralysis, and in the end the disintegration of the
dictatorship itself.

It will be necessary to plan carefully how the democratic forces
can weaken the support that people and groups have previously offered to the dictatorship. Will their support be weakened by revela-
tions of the brutalities perpetrated by the regime, by exposure of the
disastrous economic consequences of the dictators' policies, or by a
new understanding that the dictatorship can be ended? The dictators'
supporters should at least be induced to become "neutral" in their
activities ("fence sitters") or preferably to become active supporters
the movement for democracy.

During the planning and implementation of political defiance and noncooperation, it is highly important to pay close attention to all of the dictators' main supporters and aides, including their inner clique, political party, police, and bureaucrats, but especially their army.

The degree of loyalty of the military forces, both soldiers and officers, to the dictatorship needs to be carefully assessed and a determination should be made as to whether the military is open to influence by the democratic forces. Might many of the ordinary soldiers be unhappy and frightened conscripts? Might many of the soldiers and officers be alienated from the regime for personal, family, or political reasons? What other factors might make soldiers and officers vulnerable to democratic subversion?

Early in the liberation struggle a special strategy should be developed to communicate with the dictators' troops and functionaries. By words, symbols, and actions, the democratic forces can inform the troops that the liberation struggle will be vigorous, determined, and persistent. Troops should learn that the struggle will be of a special character, designed to undermine the dictatorship but not to threaten their lives. Such efforts would aim ultimately to undermine the morale of the dictators' troops and finally to subvert their loyalty and obedience in favor of the democratic movement. Similar strategies could be aimed at the police and civil servants.

The attempt to garner sympathy from and, eventually, induce disobedience among the dictators' forces ought not to be interpreted, however, to mean encouragement of the military forces to make a quick end to the current dictatorship through military action. Such a scenario is not likely to install a working democracy, for (as we have discussed) a coup d'état does little to redress the imbalance of power relations between the populace and the rulers. Therefore, it will be necessary to plan how sympathetic military officers can be brought to understand that neither a military coup nor a civil war against the dictatorship is required or desirable.

Sympathetic officers can play vital roles in the democra*
struggle, such as spreading disaffection and noncooperation in military forces, encouraging deliberate inefficiencies and the c
ignoring of orders, and supporting the refusal to carry out re

sion. Military personnel may also offer various modes of positive nonviolent assistance to the democracy movement, including safe passage, information, food, medical supplies, and the like.

The army is one of the most important sources of the power of dictators because it can use its disciplined military units and weaponry directly to attack and to punish the disobedient population. *Defiance strategists should remember that it will be exceptionally difficult, or impossible, to disintegrate the dictatorship if the police, bureaucrats, and military forces remain fully supportive of the dictatorship and obedient in carrying out its commands.* Strategies aimed at subverting the loyalty of the dictators' forces should therefore be given a high priority by democratic strategists.

The democratic forces should remember that disaffection and disobedience among the military forces and police can be highly dangerous for the members of those groups. Soldiers and police could expect severe penalties for any act of disobedience and execution for acts of mutiny. The democratic forces should not ask the soldiers and officers that they immediately mutiny. Instead, where communication is possible, it should be made clear that there are a multitude of relatively safe forms of "disguised disobedience" that they can take initially. For example, police and troops can carry out instructions for repression inefficiently, fail to locate wanted persons, warn resisters of impending repression, arrests, or deportations, and fail to report important information to their superior officers. Disaffected officers in turn can neglect to relay commands for repression down the chain of command. Soldiers may shoot over the heads of demonstrators. Similarly, for their part, civil servants can lose files and instructions, work inefficiently, and become "ill" so that they need to stay home until they "recover."

Shifts in strategy

he political defiance strategists will need constantly to assess how grand strategy and the specific campaign strategies are being lemented. It is possible, for example, that the struggle may not well as expected. In that case it will be necessary to calculate what shifts in strategy might be required. What can be done to increase the movement's strength and regain the initiative? In such a situation, it will be necessary to identify the problem, make a strategic reassessment, possibly shift struggle responsibilities to a different population group, mobilize additional sources of power, and develop alternative courses of action. When that is done, the new plan should be implemented immediately.

Conversely, if the struggle has gone much better than expected and the dictatorship is collapsing earlier than previously calculated, how can the democratic forces capitalize on unexpected gains and move toward paralyzing the dictatorship? We will explore this question in the following chapter.

NINE
DISINTEGRATING THE DICTATORSHIP

The cumulative effect of well-conducted and successful political defiance campaigns is to strengthen the resistance and to establish and expand areas of the society where the dictatorship faces limits on its effective control. These campaigns also provide important experience in how to refuse cooperation and how to offer political defiance. That experience will be of great assistance when the time comes for noncooperation and defiance on a mass scale.

As was discussed in Chapter Three, obedience, cooperation, and submission are essential if dictators are to be powerful. Without access to the sources of political power, the dictators' power weakens and finally dissolves. Withdrawal of support is therefore the major required action to disintegrate a dictatorship. It may be useful to review how the sources of power can be affected by political defiance.

Acts of symbolic repudiation and defiance are among the available means to undermine the regime's moral and political *authority* — its legitimacy. The greater the regime's authority, the greater and more reliable is the obedience and cooperation which it will receive. Moral disapproval needs to be expressed in action in order to seriously threaten the existence of the dictatorship. Withdrawal of cooperation and obedience are needed to sever the availability of other sources of the regime's power.

A second important such source of power is *human resources*, the number and importance of the persons and groups that obey, cooperate with, or assist the rulers. If noncooperation is practiced by large parts of the population, the regime will be in serious trouble. For example, if the civil servants no longer function with their normal efficiency or even stay at home, the administrative apparatus wi` be gravely affected.

Similarly, if the noncooperating persons and groups inclu those that have previously supplied specialized *skills and kn* *edge*, then the dictators will see their capacity to implement will gravely weakened. Even their ability to make well-informed decisions and develop effective policies may be seriously reduced.

If psychological and ideological influences — called *intangible factors* — that usually induce people to obey and assist the rulers are weakened or reversed, the population will be more inclined to disobey and to noncooperate.

The dictators' access to *material resources* also directly affects their power. With control of financial resources, the economic system, property, natural resources, transportation, and means of communication in the hands of actual or potential opponents of the regime, another major source of their power is vulnerable or re- moved. Strikes, boycotts, and increasing autonomy in the economy, communications, and transportation will weaken the regime.

As previously discussed, the dictators' ability to threaten or apply *sanctions* — punishments against the restive, disobedient, and noncooperative sections of the population — is a central source of the power of dictators. This source of power can be weakened in two ways. First, if the population is prepared, as in a war, to risk serious consequences as the price of defiance, the effectiveness of the available sanctions will be drastically reduced (that is, the dictators' repression will not secure the desired submission). Second, if the police and the military forces themselves become disaffected, they may on an individual or mass basis evade or outright defy orders to arrest, beat, or shoot resisters. If the dictators can no longer rely on the police and military forces to carry out repression, the dictatorship is gravely threatened.

In summary, success against an entrenched dictatorship requires that noncooperation and defiance reduce and remove the sources of the regime's power. Without constant replenishment of the necessary sources of power the dictatorship will weaken and finally disinte- grate. Competent strategic planning of political defiance against dictatorships therefore needs to target the dictators' most important urces of power.

Escalating freedom

Combined with political defiance during the phase of selective resistance, the growth of autonomous social, economic, cultural, and
political institutions progressively expands the "democratic space"
of the society and shrinks the control of the dictatorship. As the civil
institutions of the society become stronger vis-à-vis the dictatorship,
then, whatever the dictators may wish, the population is incrementally building an independent society outside of their control. If and
when the dictatorship intervenes to halt this "escalating freedom,"
nonviolent struggle can be applied in defense of this newly won
space and the dictatorship will be faced with yet another "front" in
the struggle.

In time, this combination of resistance and institution building
can lead to *de facto* freedom, making the collapse of the dictatorship and the formal installation of a democratic system undeniable
because the power relationships within the society have been fundamentally altered.

Poland in the 1970s and 1980s provides a clear example of the
progressive reclaiming of a society's functions and institutions by
the resistance. The Catholic church had been persecuted but never
brought under full Communist control. In 1976 certain intellectuals
and workers formed small groups such as K.O.R. (Workers Defense
Committee) to advance their political ideas. The organization of
the Solidarity trade union with its power to wield effective strikes
forced its own legalization in 1980. Peasants, students, and many
other groups also formed their own independent organizations.
When the Communists realized that these groups had changed the
power realities, Solidarity was again banned and the Communists
resorted to military rule.

Even under martial law, with many imprisonments and harsh
persecution, the new independent institutions of the society continued to function. For example, dozens of illegal newspapers and
magazines continued to be published. Illegal publishing houses
nually issued hundreds of books, while well-known writers boy-
ted Communist publications and government publishing hou

Similar activities continued in other parts of the society.

Under the Jaruselski military regime, the military-Communist government was at one point described as bouncing around on the top of the society. The officials still occupied government offices and buildings. The regime could still strike down into the society, with punishments, arrests, imprisonment, seizure of printing presses, and the like. The dictatorship, however, could not control the society. From that point, it was only a matter of time until the society was able to bring down the regime completely.

Even while a dictatorship still occupies government positions it is sometimes possible to organize a democratic "parallel government." This would increasingly operate as a rival government to which loyalty, compliance, and cooperation are given by the population and the society's institutions. The dictatorship would then consequently, on an increasing basis, be deprived of these characteristics of government. Eventually, the democratic parallel government may fully replace the dictatorial regime as part of the transition to a democratic system. In due course then a constitution would be adopted and elections held as part of the transition.

Disintegrating the dictatorship

While the institutional transformation of the society is taking place, the defiance and noncooperation movement may escalate. Strategists of the democratic forces should contemplate early that there will come a time when the democratic forces can move beyond selective resistance and launch mass defiance. In most cases, time will be required for creating, building, or expanding resistance capacities, and the development of mass defiance may occur only after several years. During this interim period campaigns of selective resistance should be launched with increasingly important political objectives. Larger parts of the population at all levels of the society should become involved. Given determined and disciplined political defiance during this escalation of activities, the internal weaknesses of the dictatorship are likely to become increasingly obvious.

The combination of strong political defiance and the building of independent institutions is likely in time to produce widespread international attention favorable to the democratic forces. It may also produce international diplomatic condemnations, boycotts, and embargoes in support of the democratic forces (as it did for Poland).

Strategists should be aware that in some situations the collapse of the dictatorship may occur extremely rapidly, as in East Germany in 1989. This can happen when the sources of power are massively severed as a result of the whole population's revulsion against the dictatorship. This pattern is not usual, however, and it is better to plan for a long-term struggle (but to be prepared for a short one).

During the course of the liberation struggle, victories, even on limited issues, should be celebrated. Those who have earned the victory should be recognized. Celebrations with vigilance should also help to keep up the morale needed for future stages of the struggle.

Handling success responsibly

Planners of the grand strategy should calculate in advance the possible and preferred ways in which a successful struggle might best be concluded in order to prevent the rise of a new dictatorship and to ensure the gradual establishment of a durable democratic system.

The democrats should calculate how the transition from the dictatorship to the interim government shall be handled at the end of the struggle. It is desirable at that time to establish quickly a new functioning government. However, it must not be merely the old one with new personnel. It is necessary to calculate what sections of the old governmental structure (as the political police) are to be completely abolished because of their inherent anti-democratic character and which sections retained to be subjected to later democratization efforts. A complete governmental void could open the way to chaos or a new dictatorship.

Thought should be given in advance to determine what is to the policy toward high officials of the dictatorship when its po disintegrates. For example, are the dictators to be brought to trial in a court? Are they to be permitted to leave the country permanently? What other options may there be that are consistent with political defiance, the need for reconstructing the country, and building a democracy following the victory? A blood bath must be avoided which could have drastic consequences on the possibility of a future democratic system.

Specific plans for the transition to democracy should be ready for application when the dictatorship is weakening or collapses. Such plans will help to prevent another group from seizing state power through a coup d'état. Plans for the institution of democratic constitutional government with full political and personal liberties will also be required. The changes won at a great price should not be lost through lack of planning.

When confronted with the increasingly empowered population and the growth of independent democratic groups and institutions — both of which the dictatorship is unable to control — the dictators will find that their whole venture is unravelling. Massive shut-downs of the society, general strikes, mass stay-at-homes, defiant marches, or other activities will increasingly undermine the dictators' own organization and related institutions. As a consequence of such defiance and noncooperation, executed wisely and with mass participation over time, the dictators would become powerless and the democratic defenders would, without violence, triumph. The dictatorship would disintegrate before the defiant population.

Not every such effort will succeed, especially not easily, and rarely quickly. It should be remembered that as many military wars are lost as are won. However, political defiance offers a real possibility of victory. As stated earlier, that possibility can be greatly increased through the development of a wise grand strategy, careful strategic planning, hard work, and disciplined courageous struggle.

TEN
GROUNDWORK FOR DURABLE DEMOCRACY

The disintegration of the dictatorship is of course a cause for major celebration. People who have suffered for so long and struggled at great price merit a time of joy, relaxation, and recognition. They should feel proud of themselves and of all who struggled with them to win political freedom. Not all will have lived to see this day. The living and the dead will be remembered as heroes who helped to shape the history of freedom in their country.

Unfortunately, this is not a time for a reduction in vigilance. Even in the event of a successful disintegration of the dictatorship by political defiance, careful precautions must be taken to prevent the rise of a new oppressive regime out of the confusion following the collapse of the old one. The leaders of the pro-democracy forces should have prepared in advance for an orderly transition to a democracy. The dictatorial structures will need to be dismantled. The constitutional and legal bases and standards of behavior of a durable democracy will need to be built.

No one should believe that with the downfall of the dictatorship an ideal society will immediately appear. The disintegration of the dictatorship simply provides the beginning point, under conditions of enhanced freedom, for long-term efforts to improve the society and meet human needs more adequately. Serious political, economic, and social problems will continue for years, requiring the cooperation of many people and groups in seeking their resolution. The new political system should provide the opportunities for people with varying outlooks and favored measures to continue constructive work and policy development to deal with problems in the future.

Threats of a new dictatorship

Aristotle warned long ago that ". . . tyranny can also change in tyranny. . ."[14] There is ample historical evidence from France (

---

[14] Aristotle, *The Politics*, Book V, Chapter 12, p. 233.

Jacobins and Napoleon), Russia (the Bolsheviks), Iran (the Ayatollah), Burma (SLORC), and elsewhere that the collapse of an oppressive regime will be seen by some persons and groups as merely the opportunity for them to step in as the new masters. Their motives may vary, but the results are often approximately the same. The new dictatorship may even be more cruel and total in its control than the old one.

Even before the collapse of the dictatorship, members of the old regime may attempt to cut short the defiance struggle for democracy by staging a coup d'état designed to preempt victory by the popular resistance. It may claim to oust the dictatorship, but in fact seek only to impose a new refurbished model of the old one.

Blocking coups

There are ways in which coups against newly liberated societies can be defeated. Advance knowledge of that defense capacity may at times be sufficient to deter the attempt. Preparation can produce prevention.

Immediately after a coup is started, the putschists require legitimacy, that is, acceptance of their moral and political right to rule. The first basic principle of anti-coup defense is therefore to deny legitimacy to the putschists.

The putschists also require that the civilian leaders and population be supportive, confused, or just passive. The putschists require the cooperation of specialists and advisors, bureaucrats and civil servants, administrators and judges in order to consolidate their control over the affected society. The putschists also require that the multitude of people who operate the political system, the society's institutions, the economy, the police, and the military forces will passively submit and carry out their usual functions as modified by the putschists' orders and policies.

The second basic principle of anti-coup defense is to resist the putschists with noncooperation and defiance. The needed cooperation and assistance must be denied. Essentially the same means of struggle that was used against the dictatorship can be used against the new threat, but applied immediately. If both legitimacy and cooperation are denied, the coup may die of political starvation and the chance to build a democratic society restored.

Constitution drafting

The new democratic system will require a constitution that establishes the desired framework of the democratic government. The constitution should set the purposes of government, limits on governmental powers, the means and timing of elections by which governmental officials and legislators will be chosen, the inherent rights of the people, and the relation of the national government to other lower levels of government.

Within the central government, if it is to remain democratic, a clear division of authority should be established between the legislative, executive, and judicial branches of government. Strong restrictions should be included on activities of the police, intelligence services, and military forces to prohibit any legal political interference.

In the interests of preserving the democratic system and impeding dictatorial trends and measures, the constitution should preferably be one that establishes a federal system with significant prerogatives reserved for the regional, state, and local levels of government. In some situations the Swiss system of cantons might be considered in which relatively small areas retain major prerogatives, while remaining a part of the whole country.

If a constitution with many of these features existed earlier in the newly liberated country's history, it may be wise simply to restore it to operation, amending it as deemed necessary and desirable. If a suitable older constitution is not present, it may be necessary to operate with an interim constitution. Otherwise, a new constitution will need to be prepared. Preparing a new constitution will take considerable time and thought. Popular participation in the process is desirable and required for ratification of a new text amendments. One should be very cautious about including in constitution promises that later might prove impossible to in ment or provisions that would require a highly centralized government, for both can facilitate a new dictatorship.

The wording of the constitution should be easily understood by the majority of the population. A constitution should not be so complex or ambiguous that only lawyers or other elites can claim to understand it.

A democratic defense policy

The liberated country may also face foreign threats for which a defense capacity would be required. The country might also be threatened by foreign attempts to establish economic, political, or military domination.

In the interests of maintaining internal democracy, serious consideration should be given to applying the basic principles of political defiance to the needs of national defense.[15] By placing resistance capacity directly in the hands of the citizenry, newly liberated countries could avoid the need to establish a strong military capacity which could itself threaten democracy or require vast economic resources much needed for other purposes.

It must be remembered that some groups will ignore any constitutional provision in their aim to establish themselves as new dictators. Therefore, a permanent role will exist for the population to apply political defiance and noncooperation against would-be dictators and to preserve democratic structures, rights, and procedures.

A meritorious responsibility

The effect of nonviolent struggle is not only to weaken and remove the dictators but also to empower the oppressed. This technique enables people who formerly felt themselves to be only pawns or victims to wield power directly in order to gain by their own efforts greater freedom and justice. This experience of struggle has impor

---

Gene Sharp, *Civilian-Based Defense: A Post-Military Weapons System* (Princ New Jersey: Princeton University Press, 1990).

tant psychological consequences, contributing to increased self-esteem and self-confidence among the formerly powerless.

One important long-term beneficial consequence of the use of nonviolent struggle for establishing democratic government is that the society will be more capable of dealing with continuing and future problems. These might include future governmental abuse and corruption, maltreatment of any group, economic injustices, and limitations on the democratic qualities of the political system. The population experienced in the use of political defiance is less likely to be vulnerable to future dictatorships.

After liberation, familiarity with nonviolent struggle will provide ways to defend democracy, civil liberties, minority rights, and prerogatives of regional, state, and local governments and nongovernmental institutions. Such means also provide ways by which people and groups can express extreme dissent peacefully on issues seen as so important that opposition groups have sometimes resorted to terrorism or guerrilla warfare.

The thoughts in this examination of political defiance or nonviolent struggle are intended to be helpful to all persons and groups who seek to lift dictatorial oppression from their people and to establish a durable democratic system that respects human freedoms and popular action to improve the society.

There are three major conclusions to the ideas sketched here:

- Liberation from dictatorships is possible;

- Very careful thought and strategic planning will be required to achieve it; and

- Vigilance, hard work, and disciplined struggle, often at great cost, will be needed.

The oft quoted phrase "Freedom is not free" is true. No outside force is coming to give oppressed people the freedom they so much want. People will have to learn how to take that freedom themselves. Easy it cannot be.

If people can grasp what is required for their own liberation, they can chart courses of action which, through much travail, can eventually bring them their freedom. Then, with diligence they can construct a new democratic order and prepare for its defense. Freedom won by struggle of this type can be durable. It can be maintained by a tenacious people committed to its preservation and enrichment.

APPENDIX ONE
THE METHODS OF NONVIOLENT ACTION[16]

THE METHODS OF NONVIOLENT PROTEST AND PERSUASION

Formal statements
1. Public speeches
2. Letters of opposition or support
3. Declarations by organizations and institutions
4. Signed public statements
5. Declarations of indictment and intention
6. Group or mass petitions

Communications with a wider audience
7. Slogans, caricatures, and symbols
8. Banners, posters, and displayed communications
9. Leaflets, pamphlets, and books
10. Newspapers and journals
11. Records, radio, and television
12. Skywriting and earthwriting

Group representations
13. Deputations
14. Mock awards
15. Group lobbying
16. Picketing
17. Mock elections

Symbolic public acts
18. Display of flags and symbolic colors
19. Wearing of symbols

---

[16] This list, with definitions and historical examples, is taken from Gene Sharp, *The Politics of Nonviolent Action*, Part Two, *The Methods of Nonviolent Action*.

20. Prayer and worship
21. Delivering symbolic objects
22. Protest disrobings
23. Destruction of own property
24. Symbolic lights
25. Displays of portraits
26. Paint as protest
27. New signs and names
28. Symbolic sounds
29. Symbolic reclamations
30. Rude gestures

Pressures on individuals
31. "Haunting" officials
32. Taunting officials
33. Fraternization
34. Vigils

Drama and music
35. Humorous skits and pranks
36. Performance of plays and music
37. Singing

Processions
38. Marches
39. Parades
40. Religious processions
41. Pilgrimages
42. Motorcades

Honoring the dead
43. Political mourning
44. Mock funerals
45. Demonstrative funerals
46. Homage at burial places

Public assemblies
47. Assemblies of protest or support
48. Protest meetings
49. Camouflaged meetings of protest
50. Teach-ins

Withdrawal and renunciation
51. Walk-outs
52. Silence
53. Renouncing honors
54. Turning one's back

THE METHODS OF SOCIAL NONCOOPERATION

Ostracism of persons
55. Social boycott
56. Selective social boycott
57. Lysistratic nonaction
58. Excommunication
59. Interdict

Noncooperation with social events, customs, and institutions
60. Suspension of social and sports activities
61. Boycott of social affairs
62. Student strike
63. Social disobedience
64. Withdrawal from social institutions

Withdrawal from the social system
65. Stay-at-home
66. Total personal noncooperation
67. Flight of workers
68. Sanctuary
69. Collective disappearance
70. Protest emigration *(hijrat)*

THE METHODS OF ECONOMIC NONCOOPERATION:
(1) ECONOMIC BOYCOTTS

Action by consumers
71. Consumers' boycott
72. Nonconsumption of boycotted goods
73. Policy of austerity
74. Rent withholding
75. Refusal to rent
76. National consumers' boycott
77. International consumers' boycott

Action by workers and producers
78. Workmen's boycott
79. Producers' boycott

Action by middlemen
80. Suppliers' and handlers' boycott

Action by owners and management
81. Traders' boycott
82. Refusal to let or sell property
83. Lockout
84. Refusal of industrial assistance
85. Merchants' "general strike"

Action by holders of financial resources
86. Withdrawal of bank deposits
87. Refusal to pay fees, dues, and assessments
88. Refusal to pay debts or interest
89. Severance of funds and credit
90. Revenue refusal
91. Refusal of a government's money

Action by governments
92. Domestic embargo
93. Blacklisting of traders
94. International sellers' embargo
95. International buyers' embargo
96. International trade embargo

THE METHODS OF ECONOMIC NONCOOPERATION: (2) THE STRIKE

Symbolic strikes
97. Protest strike
98. Quickie walkout (lightning strike)

Agricultural strikes
99. Peasant strike
100. Farm workers' strike

Strikes by special groups
101. Refusal of impressed labor
102. Prisoners' strike
103. Craft strike
104. Professional strike

Ordinary industrial strikes
105. Establishment strike
106. Industry strike
107. Sympathetic strike

Restricted strikes
108. Detailed strike
109. Bumper strike
110. Slowdown strike
111. Working-to-rule strike
112. Reporting "sick" (sick-in)
113. Strike by resignation
114. Limited strike
115. Selective strike

Multi-industry strikes
116. Generalized strike
117. General strike

Combinations of strikes and economic closures
118. *Hartal*
119. Economic shutdown

THE METHODS OF POLITICAL NONCOOPERATION

Rejection of authority
120. Withholding or withdrawal of allegiance
121. Refusal of public support
122. Literature and speeches advocating resistance

Citizens' noncooperation with government
123. Boycott of legislative bodies
124. Boycott of elections
125. Boycott of government employment and positions
126. Boycott of government departments, agencies and
     other bodies
127. Withdrawal from government educational institutions
128. Boycott of government-supported organizations
129. Refusal of assistance to enforcement agents
130. Removal of own signs and placemarks
131. Refusal to accept appointed officials
132. Refusal to dissolve existing institutions

Citizens' alternatives to obedience
133. Reluctant and slow compliance
134. Nonobedience in absence of direct supervision
135. Popular nonobedience
136. Disguised disobedience
137. Refusal of an assemblage or meeting to disperse
138. Sitdown
139. Noncooperation with conscription and deportation
140. Hiding, escape and false identities
141. Civil disobedience of "illegitimate" laws

Action by government personnel
142. Selective refusal of assistance by government aides
143. Blocking of lines of command and information
144. Stalling and obstruction
145. General administrative noncooperation

146. Judicial noncooperation
147. Deliberate inefficiency and selective noncooperation by enforcement agents
148. Mutiny

Domestic governmental action
149. Quasi-legal evasions and delays
150. Noncooperation by constituent governmental units

International governmental action
151. Changes in diplomatic and other representation
152. Delay and cancellation of diplomatic events
153. Withholding of diplomatic recognition
154. Severance of diplomatic relations
155. Withdrawal from international organizations
156. Refusal of membership in international bodies
157. Expulsion from international organizations

THE METHODS OF NONVIOLENT INTERVENTION

Psychological intervention
158. Self-exposure to the elements
159. The fast
    (a) Fast of moral pressure
    (b) Hunger strike
    (c) Satyagrahic fast
160. Reverse trial
161. Nonviolent harassment

Physical intervention
162. Sit-in
163. Stand-in
164. Ride-in
165. Wade-in
166. Mill-in
167. Pray-in
168. Nonviolent raids

169. Nonviolent air raids
170. Nonviolent invasion
171. Nonviolent interjection
172. Nonviolent obstruction
173. Nonviolent occupation

Social intervention
174. Establishing new social patterns
175. Overloading of facilities
176. Stall-in
177. Speak-in
178. Guerrilla theater
179. Alternative social institutions
180. Alternative communication system

Economic intervention
181. Reverse strike
182. Stay-in strike
183. Nonviolent land seizure
184. Defiance of blockades
185. Politically motivated counterfeiting
186. Preclusive purchasing
187. Seizure of assets
188. Dumping
189. Selective patronage
190. Alternative markets
191. Alternative transportation systems
192. Alternative economic institutions

Political intervention
193. Overloading of administrative systems
194. Disclosing identities of secret agents
195. Seeking imprisonment
196. Civil disobedience of "neutral" laws
197. Work-on without collaboration
198. Dual sovereignty and parallel government

APPENDIX TWO
ACKNOWLEDGEMENTS AND NOTES ON THE HISTORY OF FROM DICTATORSHIP TO DEMOCRACY

I have incurred several debts of gratitude while writing the original edition of this essay. Bruce Jenkins, my Special Assistant in 1993, made an inestimable contribution by his identification of problems in content and presentation. He also made incisive recommendations for more rigorous and clearer presentations of difficult ideas (especially concerning strategy), structural reorganization, and editorial improvements.

I am also grateful for the editorial assistance of Stephen Coady. Dr. Christopher Kruegler and Robert Helvey offered very important criticisms and advice. Dr. Hazel McFerson and Dr. Patricia Parkman provided information on struggles in Africa and Latin America, respectively. However, the analysis and conclusions contained therein are solely my responsibility.

In recent years special guidelines for translations have been developed, primarily due to Jamila Raqib's guidance and to the lessons learned from earlier years. This has been necessary in order to ensure accuracy in languages in which there has earlier been no established clear terminology for this field.

"From Dictatorship to Democracy" was written at the request of the late U Tin Maung Win, a prominent exile Burmese democrat who was then editor of *Khit Pyaing (The New Era Journal)*.

The preparation of this text was based over forty years of research and writing on nonviolent struggle, dictatorships, totalitarian systems, resistance movements, political theory, sociological analysis, and other fields.

I could not write an analysis that had a focus only on Burma, as I did not know Burma well. Therefore, I had to write a generic analysis.

The essay was originally published in installments in *Khit Pyaing* in Burmese and English in Bangkok, Thailand in 1993. Afterwards it was issued as a booklet in both languages (1994) and in Burmese again (1996 and 1997). The original booklet editions from Bangkok were issued with the assistance of the Committee for the Restoration of Democracy in Burma.

It was circulated both surreptitiously inside Burma and among exiles and sympathizers elsewhere. This analysis was intended only for use by Burmese democrats and various ethnic groups in Burma that wanted independence from the Burman-dominated central government in Rangoon. (Burmans are the dominant ethnic group in Burma.)

I did not then envisage that the generic focus would make the analysis potentially relevant in any country with an authoritarian or dictatorial government. However, that appears to have been the perception by people who in recent years have sought to translate and distribute it in their languages for their countries. Several persons have reported that it reads as though it was written for their country.

The SLORC military dictatorship in Rangoon wasted no time in denouncing this publication. Heavy attacks were made in 1995 and 1996, and reportedly continued in later years in newspapers, radio, and television. As late as 2005, persons were sentenced to seven-year prison terms merely for being in possession of the banned publication.

Although no efforts were made to promote the publication for use in other countries, translations and distribution of the publication began to spread on their own. A copy of the English language edition was seen on display in the window of a bookstore in Bangkok by a student from Indonesia, was purchased, and taken back home. There, it was translated into Indonesian, and published in 1997 by a major Indonesian publisher with an introduction by Abdurrahman Wahid. He was then head of Nadhlatul Ulama, the largest Muslim organization in the world with thirty-five million members, and later

President of Indonesia.

During this time, at my office at the Albert Einstein Institution we only had a handful of photocopies from the Bangkok English language booklet. For a few years we had to make copies of it when we had enquiries for which it was relevant. Later, Marek Zelaskiewz, from California, took one of those copies to Belgrade during Milosovic's time and gave it to the organization Civic Initiatives. They translated it into Serbian and published it. When we visited Serbia after the collapse of the Milosevic regime we were told that the booklet had been quite influential in the opposition movement.

Also important had been the workshop on nonviolent struggle that Robert Helvey, a retired US Army colonel, had given in Budapest, Hungary, for about twenty Serbian young people on the nature and potential of nonviolent struggle. Helvey also gave them copies of the complete *The Politics of Nonviolent Action*. These were the people who became the Otpor organization that led the nonviolent struggle that brought down Milosevic.

We usually do not know how awareness of this publication has spread from country to country. Its availability on our web site in recent years has been important, but clearly that is not the only factor. Tracing these connections would be a major research project.

"From Dictatorship to Democracy" is a heavy analysis and is not easy reading. Yet it has been deemed to be important enough for at least twenty-eight translations (as of January 2008) to be prepared, although they required major work and expense.

Translations of this publication in print or on a web site include the following languages: Amharic (Ethiopia), Arabic, Azeri (Azerbaijan), Bahasa Indonesia, Belarusian, Burmese, Chin (Burma), Chinese (simplified and traditional Mandarin), Dhivehi (Maldives), Farsi (Iran), French, Georgian, German, Jing Paw (Burma), Karen (Burma), Khmer (Cambodia), Kurdish, Kyrgyz (Kyrgyzstan), Nepali, Pashto (Afghanistan and Pakistan), Russian, Serbian, Spanish, Tibetan, Tigrinya (Eritrea), Ukrainian, Uzbek (Uzbekistan), and Vietnamese. Several others are in preparation.

Between 1993 and 2002 there were six translations. Between 2003 and 2008 there have been twenty-two.

The great diversity of the societies and languages into which translations have spread support the provisional conclusion that the persons who initially encounter this document have seen its analysis to be relevant to their society.

Gene Sharp

January 2008
Albert Einstein Institution
Boston, Massachusetts

APPENDIX THREE
A Note About Translations and Reprinting of this Publication

To facilitate dissemination of this publication it has been placed in the public domain. That means that anyone is free to reproduce it or disseminate it.

The author, however, does have several requests that he would like to make, although individuals are under no legal obligation to follow such requests.

- The author requests that no changes be made in the text, either additions or deletions, if it is reproduced.

- The author requests notification from individuals who intend to reproduce this document. Notification can be given to the Albert Einstein Institution (contact information appears in the beginning of this publication immediately before the Table of Contents).

- The author requests that if this document is going to be translated, great care must be taken to preserve the original meaning of the text. Some of the terms in this publication will not translate readily into other languages, as direct equivalents for "nonviolent struggle" and related terms may not be available. Thus, careful consideration must be given to how these terms and concepts are to be translated so as to be understood accurately by new readers.

For individuals and groups that wish to translate this work, the Albert Einstein Institution has developed a standard set of translation procedures that may assist them. They are as follows:

- A selection process takes place to select a translator. Candidates are evaluated on their fluency in both English and the language into which the work will be translated. Candidates are also evaluated on their general knowledge surrounding the subject area and their understanding of the terms and concepts present in the text.

- An evaluator is selected by a similar process. The evaluator's job is to thoroughly review the translation and to provide feedback and criticism to the translator. It is often better if the translator and evaluator do not know the identities of each other.

- Once the translator and evaluator are selected, the translator submits a sample translation of two or three pages of the text, as well as a list of a number of significant key terms that are present in the text.

- The evaluator evaluates this sample translation and presents feedback to the translator.

- If major problems exist between the translator's sample translation and the evaluator's evaluation of that translation, then either the translator or the evaluator may be replaced, depending upon the judgement of the individual or group that is sponsoring the translation. If minor problems exist, the translator proceeds with the full translation of the text, keeping in mind the comments of the evaluator.

- Once the entire text is translated, the evaluator evaluates the entire text and gives feedback to the translator.

- Once the translator has considered this feedback and made any necessary changes, the final version of the text is complete and the translated book is ready to be printed and distributed.

About the Author

Gene Sharp is Senior Scholar at the Albert Einstein Institution in Boston, Massachusetts, USA. He holds a BA and an MA from Ohio State University, and a D Phil in political theory from Oxford University. He has also been awarded honorary degrees of Doctor of Laws from Manhattan College and Doctor of Humanitarian Service from Rivier College. Professor Emeritus of Political Science at the University of Massachusetts-Dartmouth, he has also taught at the University of Oslo, the University of Massachusetts at Boston, and for nearly thirty years held a research appointment at Harvard University's Center for International Affairs. His books in English include *The Politics of Nonviolent Action* (1973), *Gandhi as a Political Strategist* (1979), *Social Power and Political Freedom* (1980), *Making Europe Unconquerable* (1985), and *Civilian-Based Defense: A Post-Military Weapons System* (1990). His latest major work is *Waging Nonviolent Struggle: 20th Century Practice and 21st Century Potential* (2005). His writings have appeared in more than thirty languages.

The Albert Einstein Institution

The mission of the Albert Einstein Institution is to advance the world-wide study and strategic use of nonviolent action in conflict. The Institution is committed to:

defending democratic freedoms and institutions;

opposing repression, dictatorship and genocide; and

reducing the reliance on violence as an instrument of policy.

This mission is pursued by:

encouraging research and policy studies on the methods of nonviolent action and their past use in diverse conflicts;

sharing the results of this research with the public through publications, conferences, and the media; and

consulting with groups in conflict about the strategic potential of nonviolent action.

The Albert Einstein Institution, PO Box 455, East Boston, MA 02128, USA
Tel +1-617-247 4882 Fax +1-617-247-4035 E-mail einstein@igc.org Web
www.aeinstein.org

For Further Reading

1. *The Anti-Coup* by Gene Sharp and Bruce Jenkins. Boston: The Albert Einstein Institution, 2003.

2. *Dictionary of Civilian Struggle: Technical Terminology of Nonviolent Action and the Control of Political Power* by Gene Sharp. Publication forthcoming.

3. *On Strategic Nonviolent Conflict: Thinking About the Fundamentals* by Robert L. Helvey. Boston: The Albert Einstein Institution, 2002.

4. *The Politics of Nonviolent Action* (3 vols.) by Gene Sharp. Boston: Extending Horizons Books, Porter Sargent Publishers, 1973.

5. *Self-Liberation* by Gene Sharp with the assistance of Jamila Raqib. Boston: The Albert Einstein Institution, 2010.

6. *Social Power and Political Freedom* by Gene Sharp. Boston: Extending Horizons Books, Porter Sargent Publishers, 1980.

7. *There Are Realistic Alternatives* by Gene Sharp. Boston: The Albert Einstein Institution, 2003.

8. *Waging Nonviolent Struggle: 20th Century Practice and 21st Century Potential* by Gene Sharp. Boston: Extending Horizons Books, Porter Sargent Publishers, 2005.

For order information, please contact:

The Albert Einstein Institution
P.O. Box 455
East Boston, MA 02128, USA
Tel: USA +1 617-247-4882
Fax: USA +1 617-247-4035
E-mail: einstein@igc.org
Website: www.aeinstein.org